111 POEMS

111 Poems

CHRISTOPHER
MIDDLETON

CARCANET NEW PRESS
Manchester

First published in 1983 by
CARCANET NEW PRESS LIMITED
208-212 Corn Exchange Buildings
Manchester M4 3BQ

British Library Cataloguing in Publication Data

Middleton, Christopher
   111. poems.
   1.   German poetry—Translation into English
   2.   English poetry—Translation from German
   I.   Title
   831'.914'08   PT1160.E5
   ISBN 0-85635-457-0

The publisher acknowledges the financial assistance of the Arts
Council of Great Britain.

Printed in England by SRP Ltd, Exeter

PREFATORY NOTE

This book is largely a selection of 100 poems from five books, each of which had a serial design of its own: *Torso 3* (1962), *Nonsequences / Selfpoems* (1965), *Our Flowers & Nice Bones* (1969), *The Lonely Suppers of W. V. Balloon* (1975), and *Carminalenia* (1980). The table of contents shows in which books poems first appeared.

The last section consists of 11 poems from among others written between Summer 1978 and Spring 1981.

Acknowledgment is made to the editors of the following journals, in which poems of the last section first appeared: *Lettera* (Cardiff), *The London Review of Books*, *Paideuma* (Orono, Maine), *Perception* (O. Ars, Cambridge, Mass.), *Poetry* (Chicago), *Poetry Nation Review*, *Straight Lines* (London).

CONTENTS

OBJECTS AT BRAMPTON ASH

The quick thrush cocks his head,
bunching his pectorals, halted.

Long holly shadows hone his shining claw;
you thumb its edge and grass gets grassier.

The tapered spire, at anchor in its ring
of tomb and cedar, has to quit ascending.

So you revolve in hearth-smoke's occult caves,
banished by touch of frost beading the roofs.

What increase, could these ends outlast
perpetual waste.

OYSTERCATCHERS

So luminous around them lay the air,
The wavebeat died; rocks in the bay below
Retrieved their shadows, shrank to nothingness.
And here they flew, unerringly as souls; it seemed
The body's beauty died and they remembered
Only the dazzling wrists that launched them once.
In upward vertical flight,
Black M upon white M the wings' twin boomerangs
Fought the full blast of western ocean wind.
In level flight their voices rose like flutes,
And imposed on the air a sudden shape;
Short cries, unshaded, liquid, lingering
An instant overhead and then clean gone.
That black and white, by phantom definition
Anchored in emptiness, gave, almost one supposed,
Gave off the calm so luminous around them.
As bodies they could shed all trammeling,
More eager with their shape's precision move
For having mastered so their own harsh element,
Mastered the shrouding armies of the wind,
And launched in space another, wilder song.

A speck of dark at low tide on the tideline,
It could not be identified as any known thing,
Until, as one approached, a neck was clear
(It is agreed that logs, or cans, are neckless),
And then a body, over which the neck stood
Curved like a questionmark, emerged
As oval, and the whole shape was crouching
Helpless in a small pool the sea had left.

The oval body, with green sheen as of pollen
Shading off into the black plumage, and the neck
Surmounted by the tiny wide-eyed head,
Were not without beauty. The head was moving,
So like a cobra it seemed rash to offer
An introductory finger to the long hooked bill
Stabbing the air. Danger had so
Sharpened what intelligence the bird possessed,
It seemed to pierce the mind of the observer.
In fact we were afraid, yes afraid of each other.

Finally though I picked it up and took it
To a quiet side-bay where dogs were rarer.
Here the shag sat, happy in the sun,
Perched on a slab of rock where a pool was,
In which I caught five fish for it
With a pocketknife, a handkerchief
And a plunging forefinger. But at six o'clock
It left the rock and waddled off seaward.

Though breakers came in high and curling
It straddled them, bouncing, buoyant,
Borne along the sealine sideways, with head up,
Slithering across the bay's whole width, and then
Drifted ashore again, to scuttle flapping
With webbed feet flat like a Saturday banker's
To shelter on a level rock. Here it studied,
With the air of one of whom something is expected,
The turbulent Atlantic slowly rising.
What could I do but leave it meditating?

Early next morning, on the bay's north side,
I found it cuddled under the cliff. The tide
Was low again. What hungry darkness
Had driven so the dark young shag to shelter?
It did not resist when I picked it up.
Something had squeezed the cobra out of it.

I took it to a cave where the sun shone in,
Then caught two fish. It opened one green eye,
And then another. But though I cut
The fish into portions, presenting these
To the bill's hooked tip, it only shook its head.
Noon came. The shag slept in the cave. At two
I hurried back. The shag was stone dead,
With its fine glossy head laid back a little
Over the left shoulder, and a few flies
Were pestering its throat and the fish scraps
Now unlikely to get eaten.

                    Ten minutes perhaps
I sat there, then carried it up the cliff path
And across the headland to a neighbouring cove
Where oystercatchers and hawks flew and far
Far below in loose heaps small timber lay, tickled
By a thin finger of sea. There I flung the shag,
For in some such place, I thought,
Such bodies best belong, far from bathers, among
The elements that compose and decompose them,
Unconscious, strange to freedom, but perceptible
Through narrow slits that score the skin of things.

Or perhaps (for I could not see the body falling)
A hand rose out of air and plucked the corpse
From its arc and took it, warm still,
To some safer place and concealed it there,
Quite unobtrusively, but sure, but sure.

THE THOUSAND THINGS

Dry vine leaves burn in an angle of the wall.
Dry vine leaves and a sheet of paper, overhung
by the green vine.
From an open grate in an angle of the wall
dry vine leaves and dead flies send smoke up
into the green vine where grape clusters go
ignored by lizards. Dry vine leaves
and a few dead flies on fire
and a Spanish toffee spat
into an angle of the wall
make a smell that calls to mind
the thousand things. Dead flies go,
paper curls and flares,
Spanish toffee sizzles and the smell
has soon gone over the wall.

A naked child jumps over the threshold,
waving a green spray of leaves of vine.

ALBA AFTER SIX YEARS

There was a winter
          dark fell by five
four noses ran
          and shouting children
she got so quickly in a rage.

Now when I wake
          through mist and petrol
birdsong cannonades
          blaze open-sighted
at a climbing sun.

Hopeful but prone
          I turn to face a wall
between me and that wall
          surprised to meet
wild arms which did not hold this way before.

14

CHINA SHOP VIGIL

Useful these bowls may be;
what fatness makes the hollows glow,
their shadows bossed and plump.

Precisely there a wheel whirling backward
flattens them. Knuckles whiten on copper:
headless men are hammering drums.

Cup and teapot may be such comforters:
small jaws mincing chatter
over the bad blood between us once.

When baking began, the air in jugs frothed
for milk, or lupins. Now mob is crushed
by mob, what fatness but in wild places,

where some half dozen dusty mindful men
drinking from gourd or canvas huddle,
and can speak at last of the good rain.

MALE TORSO

Before I woke, the customed thews
Alighted on strangeness.
Crammed over booms of vine,
The once buxom canvas quilled.

From his hot nest, before I woke,
The snowgoose flew, in skyward rings;
And funnelled air that filled my mouth
Rang with his wingbeat.

The customed eyes, before I woke, were glass;
A bleating queen whose legs were sheaths
Of hammered moon fed swill to pigs;
With needle oars they swept her bark

15

Through floes of starfruit, dolphins cutting
Under her eyelid's bow blue arcs in air;
And the beat of their oars like drums
Fanned my hushabye head.

Before I woke, no savour was;
But three birds sang that song they piped as girls,
Of sweetness, golden-rinded, and the fountaintree,
For mortal grapes cooled in my hands.

Then down the quartz-walled galleries of ears I coiled,
Before I woke; cymbals clashing sliced their hill,
And there with bulls my skew-wigged mother trod
Her crocus dance around its axle;

Counterwheeling Horn and Bear
Shared in her coronal the thud of fingertips on flutes,
Until my customed silence dipped and rose,
And gall was mine and darkness was.

I live now in a hutch of mud,
Without a floor, nailed by the sun,
Now for the interminable writhing sea
A fair food housed in roofless marble.

But if I wake to sniff the air of clustered stars,
I'm clothed in dew, for babes to drink,
The snowgoose moors her nest on light,
And the small horned worms walk high with hope.

SOUTHERN ELECTRIC TEDDYGIRL

Politer
And less dull than I, gazing,
Since ribs which mackintosh plates
(Belt on the ninth hole) must make,
For ease, one vertical
Brief tube, topped by a face
Eye-staring at a moon—

So Pomona, worn thin by fish and comics,
Hair yet
Bushes of torchlight
Bounding over hills through whose glades
Cool surf burrows—
Here knees and nose going
No particular way
Back, insistent, toward
Algae, plasm in pools that Pomona inched
Her million years from, now
Leaning back, on springs,
She peers for huts flash by,
Blinks with blued condescending
Eyelids over roof seas
And yellow skies that roar,
Recrossing the ankles
Her winkle-pickers bruise, to resume
Into Orpington
Her airy trail.

A BUNCH OF GRAPES

Michelangelo's Sybilla Delphica, upon what
    hard times wistfulness has fallen!
The faraway look is called a foolish thing,
    and even Rilke's girls may be lying all tousled and
tubby in bed, longing for lunch. Once though
    wistfulness meant knowing what others don't
but highly regard, seeing from a distance
    that something one contains cannot be touched.
So Goethe, coming into Italy, stopped at night
    by Lago di Garda, where he remarked
waves scrolled by south wind clutching the water
    exactly as Virgil had described them. And your
amberhaired unawakened girlchild playing
    in the park by water, in water, with a coloured ball,
was plumb constancy, in being precisely herself,
    not broken by oblivions of now and then.

Yet seeing from a distance that now and then
      can telescope, to magnify one instant into
a lilac light suffusing consciousness
      from its very ground of animal exhilaration—
this is wistfulness. One's world is multiplied,
      to share in what, the time before, was not itself,
or seemed not so. You best exist in things
      outside, are faraway, though they may not look it.
Wistfulness then is a luminous corrosive working
      through all immediate, objective, enveloping stuff
which has little or no regard for us. Suddenly
      you wake up, you swam like a fish in starlight,
and it meant what it was, the mountain pool,
      the balloon with a skin of gold that another child
hugged at your huge and crumpled bedside. And as now,
      in the panic instant, skimping responsibility,
even at wits' end, or just arranging for a journey,
      wistfulness remains, and puts the welter of things
for a time into order. It is a stillness
      nothing can sunder. It bears comparison
with a bunch of grapes on a plate on the table
      in a whitewashed room among wrinkled olive boughs
where the sun beats, and it is not yet time
      to be gone from that place.

YES, MR. BRECHT

      . . . . *Wie anstrengend es ist, böse zu sein*
                    Brecht, 'Die Maske des Bösen'

A Persian princess hangs on my wall.
In her white turban, robe of orange,
yellow slippers and white drainpipes,
I find her strange. She is alone.

A flower is in her left hand; with her right
she fingers the fan in her embroidered waistband.
On a slight hill, with deep blue sky behind,
she is musing. She may be in a paradise.

What slender symmetrical toes she too had,
that Indian girl long ago at the greengrocer's.
And even now, staring at such hopeless grace,
I have to fight, to quench a yawn.

WITHOUT SHOES

'. . . unbeschuht.' Mörike, *Peregrina*

One goes lightly
    down ignorant rays
across history buoyant
    with fruit and shade

One goes lightly
    mother and father wave
from dormer windows
    of the dove-starred house

Happy anthems—
    owls make naked
women laugh
    in the dark orchard

Babies chirping
    girls of cork
and moonboys quiver
    nailed by the bowstring

Perhaps an orange
    tastes of Padua
an alien chord
    spits visions

But one goes lightly
    over echo-dancing shores
up wrinkled lightning
    surges a friend

yielding tombs of air to trumpet wings
    along whose colonnade
without shoes
    one goes lightly.

CLIMBING A PEBBLE

What did it mean (I ask myself), to climb a pebble.
From the head of a boy depends a very thin cloud.
A red speck shifting on the Roman Campagna.
This sea-rubbed pebble has no cleft for toes.

It is simple, the ant said (my Nares and Keats).
You start low down, with caution. You need not
Slash your soles for lime like medieval Swiss.
No, but with spread arms, easing up, imperceptibly
Colluding with the air's inverted avalanche.
This cushions, O, the aching spine.

A very thin cloud is falling from the sky.
A shot, a shifting robe of crimson,
Whiffs of powder on the wind—
The sidelong buffet slams. And still you cling,
Still easing upward; giant glades, they creaked and shone,
Fresh mown, now small below—you do not smell them.

And you begin to know what it can mean,
Climbing a pebble. The paradise bird
Drops, dies, with beak fixed in the ground.
An urchin made off with its cloudthin tail.
A cardinal, with footmen to load his fowling pieces,
Peppers Italian larks a glass held spellbound.

The glass was tied to an owl, the owl to a stick.
I struck the pebble, digging, as the sun went up.

THIRST

Should wine and melon, jug and wasp
break from their images, their single sense
shine in the air, burn in the wind:
then were the ripe within grasp—
this axle of the mind.

In cooler cisterns frogs decide to sing.
How morning sun
silvered their throats in your battered pail.
How long since the dragon heard, on waking,
your footstep, heavier, cross his hill.

FIVE PSALMS OF COMMON MAN

'Je n'aime pas le dimanche'

1

Whisky whipping g-string Jaguar megaton
sometimes a 'purely rational human being'

it's me they tell of yonder sea devoid of amber
it's me they tell of column and haunting song

noncommittal me my mumble eaten
by the explosions of clocks and winds without routine

not fountains not millennia of light inextinguishable
ebbing through column and throat with its
    wombwombwomb

come my pet my demagogue excruciate me watching
yonder fountain douse the yolky dunes

The creatures of coal have looked for you all over;
the creatures of tea heard a snatch of song, it was not you.

The creatures of smoke have looked for you all over;
the creatures of tar saw a tree, it was not you.

The hand was not you, nor the hairy ear;
the belly was not you, nor the anklebone.

The eyeball was not you. Tongue and teeth
and jawbone were not you. The creatures of hair

have looked for you all over; the creatures of snow
touched a locked door, it was not you.

The creatures of paper have looked for you all over;
the creatures of steel smelled thick wallets, it was not you.

These creatures wanted to be free to look for you;
and all the time you looked to be free of their want for you.

3

W. N. P. Barbellion (pseudonymous)
March 1915
sees 'on the top of an empty omnibus
a little heap of dirty used-up bus tickets
collected by chance in the corner'

felt sick
the number of persons
the number of miles
the number of buses

at all times
the number of voices
the number of voices not speaking to one another
perplexity without surprise

Avenues Madison Shaftesbury Opéra
the number of heart beats
without number

the sick one is he on whom his desire advances asking
      why
the sick one is he who has begun all over again
not waiting not
'waiting that hour which ripens to their doom'

he speaks (Adolf Eichmann April 1961)
'in starchy, clerkish language
full of abstractions
pedantry
euphemism'

4

My blind wife kicking in her flesh of flies.
My blind wife in her ring of ribs beating me flat.
But no shard of keg shall cool my last bones.

The flies were dancing in their ring.
Their ring was dancing in the flies.
The ring desired by the nature of flies.

Stomach eyes packing it all in tight.
Knotted wings kicking in a glue film.
Ghosted in glue was the nature of eyes.

Revolt severe if sieved for its ghost of motive.
Air without motive rubbing in the arid throat.
My blind wife I warm to the coolness of bones.

5

Order imagined against fear is not order.
Saith man. Fear imagined against order

only negates or does not negate existing order.
Out of a rumbling of hollows an order is born
to negate another existing order of fear.

Nights broken before they end, interrupting
the millennia of my vigilance, saith man.
The nights of past time never slept to the end
re-enact themselves in the existing order of fear.

Another order of fear is chaos.
Images of chaos variously coordinated
by disparate imaginations accord or do not accord
to their seasons in time enacting the indeterminations.
The orders revolve in the ring or do not evolve.

The orders revolve as improvisations against fear,
changed images of chaos. Without fear, nothing.
Let me, saith man, take another look at the sea again.
And in his ear begin the rumblings of keels again.

CABAL OF CAT AND MOUSE

He has a way, the cat, who sits
on the short grass in lamplight.
Him you could appreciate, and more—
how the musky night fits him,
like a glove; how he adapts down there,
below boughs, to his velvet arena.

His, for playing in. A shadow
plodding past his white paws
could be a swad of anything;
except that, as it bolts, he retrieves
and has tenderly couched it,
and must unroll alongside, loving.

His paws dab and pat at it; his
austere head swivels at an angle

24

to the barrel neck. Prone, he eyes
its minutest move; his haunch relaxing
parades tolerance, for the pose entreats
doubly to play—it is energy

involved, if you like, in a tacit exchange
of selves, as the cat flares up again,
and has seized what he seizes.
And acts proud, does a dance, for it is
his appetite puts all the mouse into a mouse;
the avid mouse, untameable,

bound by so being to concur,
in his bones, with the procedure.
Even the end cannot cancel that.
The shift from play to kill, measured,
is not advertised. He has applied
a reserved gram of tooth power,

to raise this gibbering curt squeal
at last, and now glassily gazes down.
Plunged, barked as if punched,
and has axed his agitator. You heard
soon the headbones crunch; and you shrank,
the spine exploding like a tower in air.

THE CHILD AT THE PIANO

The child at the piano
plinking, planking, plonks.
I stare and stare. Twigs
angle the air with green outside.

Handfuls of notes, all happening at once,
her tunes do not occur; on their backs
round they whizz like stunned wasps; contour
would crush that kind of mass.

25

Telescoping flukes and faults, their
tenuous terrain dislocates
no spheres I know of. Her index rebounding
off high C beckons no hell boulder up.

The heroics, fatuous, ordain yet
this act's assumption of her whole element.
Boughs of sound swoop through the room,
happily, for her to swing from.

So I call my thought's bluff. My thumb
struts down the keys too, pings
to her plonks, on both white and black notes,
while the green air outside lets us be.

JANUARY 1919

What if I know, Liebknecht, who shot you dead.
Tiergarten trees unroll
staggering shadow, in spite of it all.
I am among the leaves; the inevitable
voices
have left nothing to say, the holed head
bleeding across a heap of progressive magazines;
torn from your face,
trees that turned around,
we do not sanctify the land with our wandering.
Look upon our children, they are mutilated.

DISTURBING THE TARANTULA

The door a maze
of shadow, peach leaves
veining its wood colour,

and cobwebs broken
breathing ah ah
as it is pushed open—

two hands
at a ladder shook
free the tarantula, it slid

black and fizzing to a rung
above eye-level,
knees jack knives,

a high-jumper's, bat mouth
slit grinning
into the fur belly—

helpful: peaches
out there, they keep growing
rounder and rounder

on branches wheeled low
by their weight over
roasted grass blades; sun

and moon, also, evolve
round this mountain
terrace, wrinkling now

with deadly green
emotion: All things
are here, monstrous convulsed

rose (don't anyone
dare come), sounding through
our caves, I hear them.

NAVAJO CHILDREN
CANYON DE CHELLY, ARIZONA

You sprouted from sand,
running, stopping, running;
beyond you tall red
tons of rock rested
on the feathery tamarisk.

Torn jeans, T-shirts
lope and skip, toes drum
and you're coming
full tilt
for the lollipops,

hopefully
arrive, daren't
look, for our stares
(your noses dribble)
prove too rude

in your silence,
can't break, either,
your upturned
monkey faces into smiles.
It's no joke,

as you grope
up, up
to the driver's door, take
them reverently, the
lollipops—

your smallest, too small,
waited three
paces back, shuffling,
then provided,
evidently

by a sister on tiptoe who
takes his hand, helps
unwrap the sugar totem.
And we are swept
on, bouncing,

look back,
seeing walls
dwarf you. But how
could you get any
more thin, small, far.

LENAU'S DREAM

Scares me mad, that dream;
wish I could tell my-
self I slept without

a dream! But what of
these tears pouring down
still, loud throb of heart?

Waking, I was done up.
My handkerchief wet
(had I just buried

someone?). Don't know how
I got hold of it,
and me fast asleep—

but they were there, the
visitors, evil,
I gave them my house

for their feast, then got
off to bed, while they
tore the place to bits,

the wild, fool ele-
mentals! Gone out now,
leaving their trail, these

tears and from tables
great wine pools dripping
slowly to the floor.

THREE BRIXTON GARDENS

In this one a boy
engages brickwork
bouncing a football—

the one-eyed house
has one, the soil just
turned for planting

a prairie, there the boy's
friend saddles up, hugs
a black twister

of hoofs at any sound
of leather
bouncing; in a third

the smell of tea,
the smell of washing make
a bit of a man

happy, happier
without vistas
of wheat or longhorn,

happiest without
the mist and its
immense animals.

GENERATIONS

On his oblong
blotting pad, indelible,
indecipherable,
a sum short of a total,
the signature doubling back—

In no hand of his, but
his father's, dead: must,
let him conjecture, identity,
here or recollected, come
to this—what sons

at the panicking
from his mouth of a call
or figure would not recoil,
all nerves,
unknowing,

or: older, needled, none
dare read in the mirror what
matter the remote
index of a will
jabbed at, dwelt on.

Never the solar track, merely
its similitudes, a rain of dreams
clubbing the gory hue
into substance, these
puzzled records of his goings-on.

The apple tree cannot trap
                    his attention. Buds
begin to uncurl; sky,
                    to turn blue,
liquidates a cloud;
                    soon fruits evolve,
on long wands flourished
                    by the bole.

For all that, little he cares.
                    The apple tree
cannot trap his attention.
                    He sticks to the bugs,
working madly in the bark,
                    as usual; to the woman,
darning his sock
                    at the heel;
to the child or two,
                    who scream in its shadow.

There are processes which are
                    not to be bothered with:
these at least illustrate
                    the effort it takes,
being a bug, darning
                    a sock, emitting
a scream. Tomorrow he flies
                    to New York with papers,

neatly typed, important; the sums
                    are already worked out
in his head. Tuesday
                    he will convince the steel
collective that the party commands
                    the wisdom of experience;
that individuals have no
                    access to this; that errors
must be rooted out.

He builds on dry ground
                for us a dwelling.
We thank him that his attention
                was not trapped by the apple
tree. Nor by the sea (since
                the apple tree only
distracts), the sea
                which we behold with wild joy,

also with fear which gnaws
                the bones of the bronzed head
he marks human as it steers
                a speck through the boiling
salt verticals, the sea
                which he ignores
and its crunching
                in the bronzed head's
blank marrow.

FOR A JUNIOR SCHOOL POETRY BOOK

The mothers are waiting in the yard.
Here come the children, fresh from school.
The mothers are wearing rumpled skirts.
What prim mouths, what wrinkly cheeks.
The children swirl through the air to them,
trailing satchels and a smell of chalk.

The children are waiting in the yard.
The mothers come stumbling out of school.
The children stare primly at them,
lace their shoes, pat their heads.
The mothers swirl through the air to cars.
The children crossly drive them home.

The mothers are coming.
The children are waiting.
The mothers had eyes that see
boiled eggs, wool, dung and bed.
The children have eyes that saw
owl and mountain and little mole.

SKETCH OF THE OLD GRAVEYARD AT COL DE CASTILLON

To get there from here you have to drop
over a dozen or more broken terrace walls;
it is the absorbed oblong far below,
sole plane on the grade of the green mountain.

There is no path down to these predictable dead
cabined in their parallels. The way up—
a track rolls off the road, and forgets itself;
antique cars chugged among the grasshoppers once,
or there were twelve shoes to shuffle under each box;
but you arrived jumping, almost out of the sky.

Their photos preserve the staring aunt;
grandpapa with a crooked smile like a locust's;
Mimi who looks beautiful and died at 17,
happy in a frock whose narrow V whittles
boneless white to the shape of a weevil's nose.

The red-backed grasshopper stuck his head,
shining, through a leaf's hole, shifting it,
little by little, the leaf, beside the blue flower.
Blue flower burying the carpenter bee.

The things one imagines of the dead,
who cannot see: broom like green porcupines,
and higher, the crab-apple tree; cold shrapnel
on the abandoned terraces; the one rose
meandering in through a wire octagon;
and cannot hear the immense murmur now,
floating behind the silence in the air.

Oval photo, dryness of the plastic rose;
hollow chapel sprayed with bullet scars.
Picking the father's bones, his flesh

tastes rotten, sticks between the teeth;
different echoes, tomb and the blue flower's bell,
thicken to old screams in the houses you explode.

And the marrow starts to itch for the sting.

And the fat daughter wore on her finger
a snail, its body transparent almost,
starry wetness, the knobbed horns taut,
pointing to the rosy mound, the tip of the finger.

THE ANCESTORS

When they come, we begin to go;
it's the ancestors,
they walk into the warm rooms,

eye our women and food, hear out
the good words. Then for words
and rooms we no more exist,

once the ancestors have come,
than a little dust on a vase,
than the breath wasted.

How do they come? They make no
parade of moans and winds;
they borrow no fears, none.

I am persuaded they have come
by the strength of shoes,
by the one shirt extra,

but if most by the bloody love
my shoes and my shirt need
to be seen that way,

I tell myself this is a thing
they'd far better not know,
who have lost the knack,

and only accuse, by the malice
they march us out with, from one
to the next lost place.

It must have been long
I lay awake,
listening to the shouts
of children in the wood.
It was no trouble, to be awake;
not to know
if that was what I was.

But I had to buy
old bottles, barter
for steerage, candles too,
each stamped with my name.
It was hurry hurry
racing the factory canal toward
the town of the kangaroo.

Up the street I came
across a knot of dead boys.
In the room with a flying bird
on practising my notes
I found its lingo;
my body knew
those torsions of the cat.

She came by, that girl,
she said it's to you, to you
I tell what they are doing
in South Greece and Germany.
My parents killed, brother gone,
they read this letter, I'll
not be here, you do not understand.

In my striped pyjamas
I was not dressed for the journey.
I changed into padded zip
jacket, boots, canvas trousers,
my pockets bulged with the bottles,
I was carrying the candles,
and I ran and I ran.

CROSSING

This is the unknown
        thing beside us. We
cross the street, walking
        together. We walk
across the street,
        and this unknown
thing surrounds us.
        It happens: to
be saying only what we mean.

Many people are
        crowding past us. This
unknown thing surrounded us. Now
        it is in us. It must have
claws, for the words
        claw their ways from
our bodies. Unless
        these are hooks we feel,
this being tenderly
        pulled against the huge stream.

We shall ignore it,
        this unknown thing. No,
do not give it a thought.
        Not now, or it cannot
keep us here, being this way
        while we can. Or it may heave
through the crowd,
        like a hope,
very destructive
        in its ebb from us.

NOTABLE ANTIQUITIES

Cooling
in the Valley of Marvels
I could see the contoured silver

prehistoric disc
of a cloud below, shaping to propel
dews into the faint folds of corn and plum,

and recall how
in Peckham where the beatle boots cost
thirty suppers of frozen cod

and shoppers
happily slice through cars and shocks
of nobody's noise,

was unearthed
some centuries ago
a Janus head, in character notable

considering
the girl's face quarried from curls one way,
the man's hard with a marble beard the other,

is no common alloy
among the models of time
so constituted, hell, the complexion rivals

even the tree
Blake surprised in Peckham, wearing
in lieu of leaves

an angel, it is said—
though how the tree took all this
is nowhere recorded.

AMOUR FOU

The hand taking the hand holds
nothing. And look: the trouble
with two sets of eyes
is that each wants out.

Islands. But we float. If face
to face we sit down in bars,
our space acquires us—
orphans of blue dust.

There is a call for help, milking
an older silence than can give suck.
Me, I shall not resist.
An owl should adore the empty air.

So make your body from the heap
of shadows down my mind. Nothing's there
for you to resist. Today, dear house,
you've not a thing that's mine.

Mirrors—not needed, we
are detached otherwise.
Chairs and shoes, our
dependants—gone.

To the call the one perplexed
voice calling replied less
and less. Darkening our room,
these are the mountains we roll.

OLD MAN, LOOKING SOUTH

Old man, looking south, you saw
these trees with pleasure; from

your toecaps their field began
rolling slopes into the hill behind.

At this gate, you said, I shall hear;
I know quite well when it's coming.

You'd even tell yourself Let's go;
and left the cottage before time.

What you saw from this gate was only
oak trees in a hollow. Not a screen:

not the old man, inoperable, mouth
a hole for air to go in and out of.

Not this tortoise mouth of a time,
pulp between the pounding gums;

at best the blades, green and jolly;
perhaps the shell's ambiguous old gleam.

Comas of the last years. Once,
sweating and naked, opening the divan

to lay the moon in white linen,
you babbled of love. Whom did you accuse?

And that you never would refuse,
benign, some book or the special talk

of work and country people, when the racking
worsened, can make me wonder still.

What hosts of things we found to say.
At this gate, looking south, up the hill;

or breakfasts in the Spring, you by then
drinking your eleventh cup of tea.

That was the same pleasure trees gave
or listening, just, for the due sound.

So one day we walked these thirty paces;
you waved and went, not looking round.

SANITY

After bolting my supper,
    eggs, sausages, bacon and chips,
I see this photograph in the paper:
    it is a crowd of ordinary people,
the Jew cocking his thatched head, the old
    vocal woman, the mechanic.

Two hold the middle of the picture:
    a young man, whose face, head-on,
has the symmetry of a dark Ajax;
    a young woman, hair anyhow,
high cheekbones, the lips parting,
    her remote eyes look straight at you.

They are walking beneath many banners.
    These they uphold casually.
The whole crowd is coming at you.
    I walk across the room, for the first time
can raise my face to the black trees,
    a silver sky of Spring.

DANGERS OF WAKING

Waking has dangers. When children
stride into the room, one by one, with reports
and messages, you shout and roll over;
but back they come, with more news,
a slamming of doors, a sound of breaking.

Like a friend you meet—what he
confides to you, you, with your empty look,
turn against him: enmity of others
who can confide nothing to anyone.
They were always the aliens,

ignored or savaged by racier children,
regretfully refused a place
in useful professions. Desirable
dead or mute or not at all,
soon every sound they heard,

voices or wheels or waters,
or wind in the barbed wires,
was the sound of a key turning in a lock.
But these dangers of waking—
well, you'll roll over, shout, do nothing,

as when the children strode in,
one by one, like Greek messengers,
to declare the killing of this or that
man, thousand, or million
on the good green sward.

ITINERARY FOR THE APPARENT DOUBLE

With you the lane winds uphill,
by day, hatching schemes;
by night, cockshut memory overhauls
your brooding mobile mind.

It steepens for you, on splay claws,
feeling the weight of eggs not engendered yet;
up the incline a lost day
floats its faint rose of shadows.

It is dark from the hill's foot to halfway up.
Boys with stones have smashed the bulbs; some shinned
corkscrewing up the posts, to rob them, furtively.
Morgue of maidenhead, *nigredo*, always foots the hill.

Here, for girls, black men come jumping
big from the ditch with naked choppers.
The mewing of owls armours them as they bolt
with goosepimples and their foretaste of moans on beds.

Yet with you the path can be picked out
from the furrow of hushed and curving space
dividing oak bough from oak bough on either side.
On the upturned face a breath of cloud and two stars.

All for you, who edge forward into the dark,
who have no mind to harp on foreterror,
trust these rounds of light, crossribbed by shade,
to be bodies, nameable, loafing against the fence.

Among them you mount the curve to the one lamp.
Here foliage hoards the spray of beams;
myriads of leaves have multiplied occult dawns.
So the beetle steals through moss in the summer night,

locked in his portable house, which he cannot enter,
and is overwhelmed by the cresting forests of chrysoprase.
You'd find it harder going, to their Cold Mountain;
always the snow cone with its ice flanks recedes,

brands in muscle the black joy of the primal motions—
mystery of effort, this seeming barely to move,
till the body, twice-born, swells with tender power,
raging afresh to expel the last stride.

It might be something, to have lived like this,
with a vacant air, behind those blessed eggs.
Yet you crossed the ridge. You have begun to drop,
free, from the zone of calm that is gorged with nothing.

Or does another day convict by the death of so many,
the slope sucking you under as you run to the choked town,
through shrieks of birds that flash in the sun like axes?
What pain you have to bring, from ignorance, always.

You flail the earth with it, you track the sun's wheel,
either way, up or down, following everywhere the hill;
the child of ashes has it for a spoon;
it domed the round Iberian tomb before Carthage came.

So you are continuous, and might have been noble;
but you will forget and I forget what you have forgotten:
how deep the hill shines under its shade of tall trees,
and when no stars come, goes to them darkly upward.

HOUSE IN THE STREET OF DOVES

So the one room was never opened,
in that house. Someone inside—
a child quietly doing a picture of a house
in the rain; only that
one room led into more never opened rooms filling
the same house.

Also in the room, a table. Through
one thick white wall a window
marvelling at a street of doves. The child put shadows,
two, across the table,
one shadow of a shouldered head, another of hair.
Empty room.

For the child has scratched out the picture;
the child walks across the room
into another, passing through many, in and out,
as if knowing the way,
stopping only a moment by the door which led then
to the street.

44

From here you could look across, and see
the house. Nobody wants it
now. Down came long demolishing shafts of sun and snow;
but we prudent bugs take
much time over the matter. Our mouths, always busy,
eat things whole.

AN ENGLISHMAN IN TEXAS

for Donald Hall

First he sees the sky. It is the one thing
not making as if to move. Far south
its blue excites the long spine
of hills. To fetch him
home from that higher tangle
could take years.

Coombs below those hills detain him. Sheep jaws
munch on berries which now ripen through
low thickets. A creek appears,
whose yellow weed foam
ephemerids populate.
Limestone belts

polished by bursts of huge rain will occur,
across trails leading him from nowhere
to nowhere. The lizard gapes
beneath a boulder,
and admits, magenta-mouthed,
the baked air

crusting some inveterate scarab. Twirl
of cardinal bird song and blue jay's
retch sculpt on space distincter
verges. Heat becomes
inhabitable, fresh fanned
from their throats.

His haze diminishes, too, when one roof
of rusting tin has topped a hollow,
as if its apparition—
manhandled—had let
at last the estranged eye in
on something.

It hardly exists. Has stuck it out by
a mere stronger irrelevance than
the horned goat skull's candid gaze
levelled at his gaze
across curly miles of scrub.
Prickly pear

looks like a telling friend for time's cripple.
Dwarf cedars thronging undulations
balk grass and buckwheat between
those hills and his place;
so each dawn, like milk, they leave
his new wish

to be present, now, to drop character,
its greed for old presences, its dirt
fruiting demi-selves in groves.
Yet there still he prods
that suture of hill and sky
for ways through . . .

Help him, tall shades, Wallace and Westfall, whose
addresses, inconspicuously,
changed as men flocked round and round
your cockeyed cabins,
bleating and sad, agog at
the gun's wit.

Or do not help him. But let him move once,
free, of himself, into some few things.
Sky, after all, meets nothing.

And with my snake axe
I'll trudge to meet him, should he come
without you.

THREE MICROZOIC NONSONNETS

for Hans Vogt

1

Failing: to sit
by the knotted hands
    the night through,

    all
        meaningless, as
the backs of words, the black
    cream of moments—

    then, on the feet,
to approach
        a door, before switching
    off,

        to put straight
a picture on the wall, the hand
    opens . . .

2

Then Goethe, he
says: The old story—
        sea-bed (from

this
      height down upon
Weimar), the whales playing,
   villages now;

   what thought of us,
our molluscs,
      had the sea-mew then; yet,
   think,

      hear him cross
again this mountain, his wingbeat
   not far.

3

. . . vines, thick with fruit,
moons of pollen &
      the wild rose

   cling,
      I make them, to
the archivolts; lion,
   cathedral snail,

   camel, my loves
make in me
      a room, growing; as light
   swells,

   propels all
night old ribby shadows up red
   curtains.

AVEBURY: THE TEMPLE

What these stones are,
stone by stone,
their circle, the road
bisecting it, and the heavy
green earthwork

Night here, gradual stars,
the dew keeps rising
in a mist till the blue
and dark beeches go
for another time another green

We sleep under a mountainous
parsley stick, its rosettes and fans
catching the dew light, and darkening
with the dreams we do not have

All night a murmur and the feet
freezing soundlessly, sleeping bags
damp, not with the tears we do not shed

And at dawn we are walking
under the sweet lime trees, we climb
a gatepost of granite and sit up there

We gaze for horsemen to come,
girls with bacon,
and among grasses for the small flowers,
the far stones touching a remoteness
which is our remoteness, stones
we ask nothing of, as they are revealed

We are revealed in our hands
holding other hands

For once not scared they will come
up the road,
others who do not know what this night is,
who do not care what comes
when the night goes, the night goes

MEROPE

Don't let me
chase
the big stone
down the mountain

your laughter
wells
here,
little spring.

BIRTH OF VENUS

```
V  V  V  V  V  V  V
 V  V  V  V  V  V
  V  V  V  V  V
   V  V  V  V
    V     V
     V  V
      V
```

VICTORIANA

In the gardens of Windsor Castle
walks a philosophic owl;
wingtips clasped over his coccyx,
stooped he stalks, pondering much.

Meanwhile the moon puts pale fire
in the turrets of Windsor Castle:
shut windows halt its gleam,
the queen is pulling her boots on.

The moon is evident also
on the buttocks of stallions grazing,
in the lake without any holes,
in the blood that drips from the owl.

For certainly blood drips down
the philosophic owl:
he leaves a pool on the turf,
wherever he stops to think.

Now the queen comes riding, sag-jawed,
down the long moonlit avenue;
her dead prince gallops beside her
on a very noble ostrich.

THE ARMADILLOS

You suddenly woke and saw
on the bedroom hearth an apple green
puddle of moonlight. It was the armadillo,
sitting on top of the chimney, put it there;
with his long snout for a siphon, I suppose.

More often the armadillos
perch in the trees. They stare
at each other, count the rings
which buckle them in; or—
they discuss things.

Don't fall, Harriet! Arthur, don't fall!
We can't help it if the armadillos
drop like bombs and catch only
in the lower branches with their claws.
Falling like that, they can't be lonely.

Winters, they leave the trees and trundle
to the end of the valley. In twos and fours
they cluster there and comfort each other.
The frost feels them under their bucklers;
they taste it happening in their jaws.

But in the trees where they build hides
of cardboard boxes and paper bags,
their main concern is believing summer.
For my friends broken by special committees
I hang out armadillo flags.

They run fast and go underground
where silence is, for sending signals.
Or they climb to the tops of telephone poles
and jam the exchanges of political assholes
with the terrible sound of knitting.

If you wake again, do not scare,
but wonder at the armadillos;
they'll be watching us from up there,
winking their neat eyes, arranging their faces,
hoping that something shows.

BONNARD

Does the body rest against his eye, the cool
changing its colours: rose, purple, silver
framed in a door, the enamel of a bath

their life the elements dream through,
figures all facing at different angles
do not touch, they include one another—

dwelling on a thing, the eye feeds its boutons
energy sprayed from a few co-ordinates: loaf & horse,
each its own dimension in the starred dream

shields the colours! blue skins,
cocooned girl's crotch, or aloof apple,
a buffoon child, flowers in a bowl

& her face everywhere, turning from a cup
to smile with a mouth like a slice
of baby watermelon, celestial clown girl

or bored, sprawling bare on a rumpled bed,
brown arm thrown across her ribs,
the left hand tilting a small breast—

but where the skin starts it is the idyll
playing out any boundary to scan
throbbing ascensions in the space around,

street dappled with skirts & metal,
woodland blue with edible branches,
crimson billow of a kitchen cloth

it is where the dogs do battle,
canaries roast in evacuated rooms,
the history-makers unload their dead,

hack it to pieces. To pick it up again,
restore it, whole, a lifetime on fingertips
grinding a rainbow from the ignorant dew.

THE CHILDREN AT LONGBOAT KEY

We have gone to the sea at evening.
We float over waves in a rubber tyre.
Your legs are glistening your hair is wet.
My shoulders are cool I hear the ripples.

Orange cloud swells over a thin black line.
We gaze at the water wheeling with rainbows.
We lean back with upturned faces.
Your hair hangs down it darkens the water.

We are floating out to sea we are happy.
On the far white sand are two black dots.
White sand curves a warm banana.
A swept and sharp banana a sword.

We see the two black dots are waving.
Bigger it grows all the sea around us.
They wave and shout we wave and wriggle.
We beat the sea with our feet and hands.

It is a very old man and a very old woman.
Far off he is jumping on the hard sand.
Far off she is brandishing a parasol.
He wears a black hat and she white stockings.

We have ridden the billows and watch the foam.
Soft crystals cling and spit on the rubber.
There are two voices shouting and mixing.
We stand in the water we feel its pull.

It is pulling your knees and you go under.
I catch your feet it is hauling you away.
The little old people walk toward us.
The sand nudges between our toes.

His black hat rim sits level over his eyes.
Her white stockings cover two sticks.
They are saying to us their big worries.
They make their hands go up and down.

We hear the voices we hold the tyre.
Its cool ring slaps to the sand between us.
They walk away in their twiggy skins.
The shrunken faces will speak no more.

They meant it well the old people.
The sea pounds the beach behind us.
Its blue roar begins like a shiver.
We watch them vanish into thin air.

PAVLOVIC VARIATIONS

1

I came to the sea shore to hear speeches about beauty.
Nobody's here.
It still gives the pebbles gooseflesh
merely to think of the metamorphoses:
driftwood sparser, modesty
after all the big words.

I came to the city, back
to the wise & their logic.
Fish met me on the way,
we walked along together.

Sea roads & city roads all lead to the same banquet.
On the table the cuts of sun are transparent & cold.
I keep watch at the gate, to discover who makes the changes in
                                                    things.
I raised my hand, to make sure of the sky:
I touched the breast of a giant bird,
dead, only it had not hit the ground.
Through its eye I saw ships travelling in circles;
an ancient way to bury the sails.
What day of creation is it?

The chair I sit on sinks deeper and deeper into the sand
under the weight of the city I am clasping.
I preserve it in the hollows of my hands like a sip of water,
with few words,
& shall surrender it to someone with fewer
tomorrow.

More & more one loves
the man beneath the sea.

2

Senator Dogface demanded a complete bomb
to rub out the problem on his agenda.
Professor Quorum, on efficient feet, strides outdoors,
behind him a trail of neatly beheaded pupils.

I numbered the pebbles: there were too many.
The sea keeps coming at me, with confusion but no change.

Moving my chair back I turn to the gate:
brown city with choked arteries; a thousand
died on paving stones under four inches of snow,
under four miles of Senator Dogface's blotting paper,
under Professor Quorum's electric pyjama cord.

I keep watch at the gate. Who makes the changes in things?
The cuts of sun thickening multiply,
young pigs & cows go gallivanting—

a summer fish patrolled its pool.
                What night waits for them
with its dioxide oven? On what day
will their creation come?

Shining yellow:
    cyclones
  polish the sea.
    Bald clown
down there, it put a stop
   to your wrinkles.

I was discovering your games:
    temple columns
shuffled by artillery,
  floating hair of the dancers;
    flute note remote foghorn
calling through surf-thunder.

The sea from its pocket
  has taken papers: unstamped,
portraitless.
   These tongues are torn from our heads, we pound
at the gates with ammunition & whiskey.

He
walks because he is not stopped by anything.
He considers things
as points breaking the light for his amusement.

Over a splintered pine these blank pages riffle.

From foam the orbiters rising; later, keel tracks,
fisheries; last, the naming of stars. With newborn mouth
a tablet sucked holy milk: I understand

the central nervous system of Alexander. I collect
25 different vine-tip sections in the camote patch. I interrogate
the quiver of needles tracking Mars.
       I can peel
an orange in 11.52 seconds. I know

nothing. The beat of a heart tears it from the breast
of the giant starry bird. Nobody
is here. Nobody knew

what to do with it.

5

To what space do they belong, the figures torn from a fog
    & what are you? A cathedral. I woke to the silver trickle
from one tap in one hut the twenty of us

    & stood up another day
lidless brimming excrement bucket
      columns & motes tearing asunder the stored deluge of
                                    light

200 metres to the bodies we dug out with bare hands
    a snowy braid was widow Lautmann
Pavel's child came to pieces in my hands.

    To what realm do they belong, rays modelling
the chevelure of stone, pierced volumes which walk
    my body through transfigurations of the rays, 200 metres
                                    more

carting the flesh in barrows
    flesh peeling from bone as we dragged them ghostless
out of the earth to the furnace

    To what region where the forms dwell all day another day
for dragging by the hair we had stroked
    ghostless bundles of flesh bulletmarks in the neck

silhouettes: to what space will the trickle from one tap scrape
    from our eyesockets the memory of that flesh, washing
the smell from our gums with a sip of water

There is one who shouts with the shape of himself
last seen
feeding on garbage in the camp near Voronezh

Now I shout with the shape of myself to hear
in the new light the flap of old timetables
platforms I spent the better part of my life on
a solitary overcoat among broken signals
& shall bleed to death on a street between the painted lions

I came to the sea shore to hear a different rampage

The city cupped in my hands I drink its terrible child gaze
Balls of foam blown inland
I found the marble head, butchered its eyesockets
& stare back at the abyss closing & opening
its immense sex

But it is now, at the table, as we whisper with things
under the old lamp that hangs

It is now
over the glass blue pepper-pot that stands, Pavlovic, stands

When we see a grass blade bend in the new light
When we can hear
someone playing a saw over the hill.

Note: the first section is a translation via German of a poem by the Yugoslav poet Miodrag Pavlovic.

THE MEASURE

She is going down to the water
restless
& the long hair on her shoulders

the arches of her feet
skinned roots of olive, as delicate,
shape small hollows of air across the sand

Clambering towards her
the sea that knows nothing
the young form, aerial, always cool hands
how do I know her

crossing with swift transition
sometimes, Ionia, your hills

it is the measure
outpacing prediction, we must go
ten thousand miles to the broken statues

THE FIND

What to do
here, now
but write

how it is
to wait, in the body
a thing keeps

pounding, biceps
grind,
almost, with

the load of it, no
need to say
who, ever.

To shed it into
an image,
how pathetic. Look:

the hero, no
bigger than
a pin, so far,

he leaps horizons,
triggering acute
crises in nature,

e.g., a man who eats
bats,
the fleas & all,

or a mountain
of a man
with his ores,

off him cascade
in chaos
glorious adventures.

This table keeps
my legs buckled,
I am hungry,

I am rock,
useless, altogether
useless, but

for waiting.
When you come,
you'll find me

gone, waiting
elsewhere, in
some brooch pin,

or in the glass
you have filled
to drink from.

SHOREHAM WALK

We walked
up through the wood
nettles & oak
a dark green

fall of light
leading us
past soft
erect wheat

then the white
potato flowers
& flints, a few
rusty can tops

it is the shining
June day, warm
as seldom
in our country

on our skin
a south wind
silver barley ears
are swaying

swaying us
& a lark
less visible than
the flower, blue

big, no bigger
than your pupil
under crusty
oaks again, ferns

they smell of salt
curved seawaves
& a place
we found

called the kingdom
of children
you said, because
nobody frowns

as you climbed
vanishing up
a giant beech, red
as old blood

tall as the sky,
so many strong
branches it
was easy

MAN ON THE WALL

up there, climbing the wall
where he is, we see him
flex the left knee
right leg straighten, right arm
sprung from the shoulder blade
left hand like a fist
of ribs

the flat body so taut
its tallness, all reek & sinew
ignores the feet his
bloody finger ends
& gasps cannot reach

but the wall
neither smooth nor rough
neither brick nor glass
horizon of schist
upright in a reversed
world not a world

there being no roof for it
to taper into
there being beyond this place
which is no place
nothing

& the legs & the arms
slip at the ultimate
tension, like liquid
the whole body subsiding
without thunder
the head out of sight
flipping back, just once
has hammered on something

we have fitted him
into the black bed the black bed
a soft whistling
as the body threshes
under the wool & the linen

CURBARAM

Curbaram says: At present they are encamped outside the walls, and we shall drive them back into the city. From this hill you can count their horses, unsaddled, in the enclosure to the left, also their tents, including the storage tents, which are not round but square. One thousand four hundred and thirty two men spread over an area of one mile: by eleven thirty they will be concentrated at the city gate, a tumultuous mass of armour, horses, elbows and heavy feet. At that time you will stop firing and save your ammunition. They will kill one another as they try to press through the gate. By noon we shall have them inside the walls, and they will see us, crowding these ridges with our camels and artillery. The rocket batteries will be positioned at these three points, northwest, south and east of the city. You will maintain a heavy and constant fire from shortly after noon until the sun sets.

Some of these men will plan to escape from the city after nightfall. They will lower ropes from the parapets, and arrive at the foot of the west wall one half hour after midnight. Probably they will be called Guillaume, Albric and Wido, but you need not concern yourselves with that: besides, there will be others, of whose names I am not yet certain. Well now, these men, about twenty in number, having reached the foot of the wall, will move stealthily westwards, making for the sea. The terrain is not easy. By three thirty their exhausted boots will have given up on them, the soles torn away by the rocks which carpet the entire area west of the city to within half a mile of the sea shore. They will continue to move forward barefoot, then on their hands and knees. By dawn, their hands, feet and knees will be lacerated down to the bones, but they will keep moving, for at dawn they will, at last, get a first sight of the ships. The ships are manned by their own people, sailors from Akra Korakas, Archangel, Florida and Plymouth. Then they will be standing, kneeling and lying on the shore, perhaps even feeling the sea as it cools their wounds and stings their eyes. At that moment, the sailors will up-anchor and cram on sail, for they will be subjected to a concerted attack by our air and sea forces: the galleys from coves north of Port Saint Simeon, carrying archers and cannon, and aircraft loaded with bundles of our widely read literature. The ships will attempt to escape, while they, for their part, will stand on the shore, shouting and waving and weeping with the pain of their wounds and their worstedness. Their ships will consequently be destroyed, as soon as their sailors have seized the opportunity to study our discharged literature.

The men on the shore will then retreat to the low dunes, where, human strength being not easily exhausted in times of stress, they will build a defensive wall of sand, rocks, seaweed and rotten fish. The wall will be fifteen yards long, three and a half feet tall, and two feet wide. It may, even at noon, provide them with a modicum of shade.

THE EAGLE

Born among the bleak immensities of the Urals, the eagle rapidly acquainted himself with towered cities of the south, whence issued on summer nights the music of mandolins, and with the cities in the northern snows, made luminous by the lanterns attached to sleighs as they travelled, with much ringing of bells, from palace to palace. His soaring flights took him also westwards, among other peaks, and it was here that his days were defined by the long notes of alp-horns creeping around the bluffs, pouring along the deep valleys, as the breath of some hatless peasant pressed into the brass mouthpiece. These were his first journeys, long journeys: from them he would return to his perch, to gaze down upon the earth below, as if its many layers of rocks and epochs were the staves of his musical score, over which his notations were beginning to spread, and his silences, in amongst and all around the striking of drums.

From the altitude of his flights he was able to discern the streets and interiors of towns hidden in the folds of time: pewter jugs, copper pans, and bottles of ruddy antique glass; Punch on muleback crossing a cobbled square, and singing, as the sun began to rise, of Silesian girls capacious as barns; a royal courtyard criss-crossed by freshly trimmed trees in which oranges flowed and dancers who sprang from shadow to shadow; in Famagusta, amid celestial flutings, the birth of a waxen-fingered Baby Saint Barnaby reducing to powder the temples of Aphrodite; and Theodora's witty but antecedent rape of a sibilant Dancing Master, Asterius by name, in a nook which housed at that time the celebrated Byzantine astrolabe.

Much later came the period of the interviews. The merest suggestion of a phrase, and he would circle the sky above with expressive swoops, plunge full tilt at his nomad interrogator, and at the last moment rise again with a gentle exertion of his powerful shoulders and vanish in a flash of russet and gold. And yet he bafflingly alluded to his caducity, and to his dealings with physicians and cupboards stacked with pots of jelly. From Ireland and France came the main sources of his sustenance; he refused the excitements of the cactus or of chemical foods and powders from the Orient.

His last flight is still a subject of lively inquiry. From a certain altitude one morning he descended on to the back of a whale, which immediately set out for Tierra del Fuego. The eagle's claws were firmly, if not desperately, planted in the black fat on the back of the whale. The whale kept to the surface for the first day and night, but at noon on the second day it submerged, despite anxious cries from the eagle, and despite the eagle's rappings on the flanks of the whale with his powerful wings. Under the sea, the eagle for the first time saw the shoals of sunfish dispersing like clouds as the whale crashed through them, and, looking back, these same shoals coagulating again as if no more than a breeze had passed. The eagle's only nourishment that day was a young mullet, who had approached the scene mistakenly.

The whale surfaced at night, but by this time the eagle no longer had any memory, his soul absorbed nothing new, except for the rushing of the water as it flowed unendingly over him. Even on the surface again, under that full moon which shone upon the two of them, he knew only this rushing, no longer the nourishing air upon his plumes, no longer the cool gusts that blew among the homely peaks and sustained his circulations and shaped his cries. This new rushing was amorphous, a blue suction dragged the great body ruthlessly into a hole which was too small even for a human hair to pass through. His feathers fell away, and his flesh; but still the claws gripped the back of the whale, and the eagle still followed every motion of the whale, rising and dipping, rolling and winding, on his regular course to Tierra del Fuego. The skeleton of the eagle is still there, the claws rooted in the black fat of the whale, the bones polished white by the rushing of the waters. The beak is wide open, as if uttering a last cry, the last of all possible cries, which is the silence. Whenever the whale rolls, the skeleton swings this way or that, with a slight clamour, something like a rattling, say, of giant leaves against the window in a dry October.

THE HISTORIAN

Things might not be so bad if I did not always have to write it in a hurry. The historian, after all, should move at a leisurely pace among the objects of his investigation, as a dog might, in a forest of lamp-posts, a lucid dog, that is, one who knows the pleasure of dragging pleasure out. What a magical forest this history has been, even then: first I wrote the official history of the trees, singly and in their concert, the wars, laws, public achievements and transactions, in the manner bequeathed to me by my illustrious forebears. Then, as my hours of sleep grew shorter, with anxiety more than with age, I set about writing the Secret History, at night, as I have indicated, when the servants were asleep in the cellars, only a few shouts in the street below, but still in fear of that man in the black raincoat, belted and hatted, who would one night appear in my doorway and ask, with his smile: "Working late again, Procopius?"—and then I would have no time to stuff my papers under the flagstone beside my littered, but not inhospitable, writing-table.

What more can be said of that girl and the two valets whose tongues were cut out, whose bodies were chopped into little pieces, packed into sacks and dropped into the sea? What of the poet expelled from the city, living now in the woods (with his second wife)—when he told the story of his friend's ludicrous funeral, the coffin too heavy, the factions struggling with flags and wreaths to claim the corpse as an advocate of their particular lies, was he laughing or crying?

I wrote the Histories in order to buy time for the writing of the Secret History. And the Secret History had to be told in a hurry; I cannot exist in this suspense for long, though it can be, for an old man, almost as exhilarating as an early love-affair, all the same. How two-faced one is, especially when facing oneself. The doctor says that I am ill. Yes. They said this of that other poet, in whose will it was written: "Let no man say that I perished because of some sickness during these years. It was their brutality which killed me, the torment of their lies, the fear which stopped my heart whenever a door would creak".

I remember Theodosius well, not a pleasant fellow, to be sure; but it was an injustice to tie him up in that cell like a donkey, with the tether tight around his throat, four months at a manger, standing there in his excrements. Once he had gone safely mad, they let him go; and he died. I am told that Theodora used to come and bray at him, when she could find the time, lift up her skirts and wiggle her bottom at him; and she had him flogged if he declined to look at her: lack of due respect.

I cannot help laughing when I think of the astrologers whom they mounted on camels and drove through the streets for the mob to jeer at. Old men. Justinian's face is said to turn, at times, into a shapeless lump of flesh: no eyes, eyebrows, nose or anything. To think of that lump buzzing with plans for the killing of thousands. They uproot entire populations, weeping children, the tenderness of old women, worshippers of different gods, gods of the streams, winds, of the earth, and march them at planting-time from their villages into faraway camps of special huts where there is nothing to do but die. No, he does not even plan it. He does whatever comes into the lump, according to the circumstances. In the name of the laws. For the acquisition and storage of riches. For the few and no questions. It all makes the young men and women somewhat more irrational than is good for our society. Our society is probably destroyed, anyhow. Never again to sleep, never again to screw, in security. Was he laughing, or was he crying, that man in his hide-out, when he told the story of the funeral?

It is still mysterious here, still real, here in this room of mine. They are still clattering about down there in the street.

Tomorrow the blue dust will go on rising, the new towers along the sea-shore too, built there to shove back the sea which licks at their palaces. The thought still bothers me, that, instead of writing, I might have changed the

THE BIRTH OF THE SMILE

There are three legends about the birth of the smile, each relating to a different epoch. It is the custom to tell these legends in a reverse chronological sequence, as if this might hopefully point toward an ever-receding antiquity with secrets which may one day be told in legends that still have to be discovered.

The first legend concerns the Sumerians. These people came down from the mountains to the plains, in search of food and water. After several centuries of food and water they became bored with the flatness of the plains, pined for the ancient exertion of striding up and down mountains, and decided to build a mountain of their own (there could be no question of returning to the old place). For ten years the men laboured at the mountain. It was the priests who put the finishing touches to it—drilling weeper-holes, planting a tree on top, fashioning chambers inside, near the base, for library materials and, inevitably, a toilet. While the priests were getting busy, an enormous sheet, woven during these ten years by the women, was draped around the mountain. Finally, everyone assembled; and then the mountain was unveiled with due ceremony and with a great beating of gongs. As the sheet sank to the ground, the strings having been cut by some excessively large pairs of Sumerian scissors, the mountain stepped fresh and naked out of its veilings, and all the Sumerians smiled for the first time. This was a short smile, all the same. The Sumerians had built a mountain to walk up and down, a mountain of the heart, a mountain of despair, a mountain of pain; but their smile disappeared when the officiating priest, from under the tree at the top, declared: "This place is a holy place; for whom it is intended, do not ask. And do not enter or climb around on the outside either, or you will die."

70

The second legend tells that the smile was born on the face of the first woman when she stood for the first time before the first man and perceived the silence with which his phallus grew and rose at the pleasure of her presence.

The third legend tells of an epoch which must have preceded that of the second, if only by a few days. This is what the legend says. When the shaper of life was making men and women, he was careful to give them strong contours to contain the spirit in them. There was always the danger that these forms might dissolve into the flowing which goes through all things. The spirit raged in the new beings, wrathful at being contained, and after mighty strainings and heavings it burst out in fire. The fire streamed from the bodies of the creatures and all creation might have been consumed, had it not been for a cool god who took the spirit in hand. Suddenly he was standing there, in front of a girl. As they faced each other, an island of coolness was created in the midst of the burning. As he gazed at the girl, he began to marvel at her lightness and grace, and at the diaphanous body from which the fire was spreading in great lashes. The god spoke divine words to her body, as he gazed in wonder. While he was speaking, the spirit overheard these words and for the first time began to grow content in such a dwelling. That was when the girl smiled. In those times, a smile was simply the consent of the spirit to dwell in us.

If older legends are ever discovered, they may explain to us the terrified smile of Kafka; or the smile inserted at the corners of Ché Guevara's mouth by the thumbs of his murderers.

A CART WITH APPLES

In the blue shadow
alone with its rose
and full of fields
round ones and yellow ones
an apple stands

a blue apple stands
in the field of yellow
alone with its cart
and round of roses
full ones and shadow ones

and full of yellow
the shadow stands
alone with an apple
a rose one a round one
in a blue field

and in the apple shadows
blue ones and yellow ones
a cart stands
alone with its field
and full of rounds

but in the field of roses
and full of apples
yellow ones and round ones
a blue cart stands
alone with its shadow

BRIEFCASE HISTORY

This briefcase was made on the Baltic coast
in 1946
some prize pig was flayed for the leather
metal stripped from a seaplane
silk for the stitching picked from parachute cord

People say where did you get that singular briefcase
and then I notice it
people ask how much did it cost
and when I say fifty cigarettes not many understand
once the leather was flying wrapped
around seaplane fuel tanks the space between
wadded with two inches of rubber
this briefcase might stop a bullet I wonder

For twenty-five years I have carried in it
books of poems battered or new
cosmic mountain notebooks plays with broken spines
bread and cheese a visiting card from Bratislava
and a pliable cranny for anything to be pocketed
at the last moment

The handle ribbed with stitches of parachute silk
anchored by clasps of seaplane metal
is worn shiny and dark with sweat
the whole thing has an unspeakable gray colour
running a fingertip over a surface
leprous one might say
various tones of gray flickering mould green
the scored leather looks to me like the footsole
of an old aborigine bowman earth in a space photo
nerve webs of a bat's wing

The two side pockets have their seams intact
two straps happily slip through buckles and hold there

Furthermore this briefcase has contained
a dynasty of shirts mostly now extinct nothing to declare
my Venus relics old stones believed
animal figures carved back of beyond in France

Everywhere
this briefcase has been with me somehow
I find reason to celebrate it today

Briefcase helping friend
ploughshare beaten from the sword
briefcase bag of tricks peaceful seaplane spirit
ocean wanderer
you have never contained an explosive device
never have you contained an explosive device
yet

PETRARCH'S COUNTRY

This peak infuriating the winds
this valley fluting down the foothills
these crabby oaks & soon apple trees & blue grape

at the valley's other end a slope of roofs
this maze long abandoned by the tinkling animals
old stone room inhaling all the winds

antique prayer book this decrepit bible
black dented bowler with a cracked brim
a lexicon of place names coming to pieces

dead or alive someone forgot the sunday trappings
but the bowler fits I clamp it on my head
under this peak a thousand weathers flow from

books in hand & looking solemn enter the Café Pons
now my full glass of wine I raise for silence
now I drink to all the winds

SNAKE ROCK

Tall snake without strut or buttress
snake which talks in the rhythms of chemicals
snake with legs

tell me where the spyholes are
come between my sheets and just be yourself
snake with two breasts which look at me

snake with hair and very tender armpits
show me the moon
show me the moon or must I split your skull
tell me

tell me animal with fruits
animal of celluose and lignin come into my house
animal with leaves
cambium animal come into my house

animal which sucks minerals out of the dirt
tell me animal drinking the sun
dead centered animal shaping sugar into wood

drinking lakes also towering flower
tell me how you can change the sun into yourself
flower with a snout
rock with claws come into my kitchen
tell me how you can cook the air and crunch its bones

flower with fur
flower with padded feet smelling of incense
snake who stands in the suchness of silence
come to my table of wood and wickerwork

flower with white teeth
calcium flower teach me the revolution
rock with jaws which bite the flies and all flesh
tell me tell me the rain

snake with a wet nose tell me the lightning
tree which snorts and twitches
umbel snoozing with bristles of soft wire

flower which runs across the street suddenly
tell me how you die
tell me how you die without having to think of it

IN BALTHAZAR'S VILLAGE

Voices in the night
            voices below begin
                        wind rising orderless too
rumbles & howls

upstairs a silver light
            falls
                        on collected rocks
& new maroon espadrilles

in another room
            Rampal's flute is
                        Bach who breathes for these
elementary propositions

odd as it is to care
            anyhow for things
                        their mass & contour
& all beginnings

OVAL HISTORY POEM

Stalking the deep
seashell
twists of a cavern below ground
he longs for an arrow
paradise capsule
flaked as the blue intact
sphere of day
outside

Puzzle
floors impenetrable rock
green breves
dapple rump to rump
these horses in a frieze
two like toy
star charts yield
not a one he can detach

Attractive
holes repulsed each pointing
finger tip
the bloodcoloured
bison lift
flighted hoofs
in a shower of earth sweat

But
thwong
the shaft still
is shivering—watch him redhanded
pluck at it
the fresh cleft
drilled in his brittle
nobody's head

MANDELSTAM TO GUMILEV 1920

The word, you said, stars in terror of it
Clung to the moon; eagles folded their wings;
Men ringed it with number, dreading its radiance.

Our sounds, woven of that radiance, were sacred,
You said—but now what a stink of dead words:
Dead bees, old hive deserted.

So take from me, I ask you, for the joy of it,
A drop of sun, a drop of honey: this
Persephone's bees ordain that we should do.

There's no unmooring the same boat twice over.
Fur-shoed shadow, certain things not a soul can hear,
Or overcome—the fear we live in, thick forest.

What's left to us? Only kisses,
Little bees, all shaggy, in their hives;
They fly into the open—their flight is death.

Night, forest of glass, the space they swarm through.
Taygetos, mountain forest, there they are born, bees
That feed on moments, honeyflower, and mint.

So take this gift, for the joy of it, this
Necklace, unassuming, made of dead bees:
They wove the honey, wove it back to sunlight.

HOLY COW

No, you never give us
a thought. Indifferent, down
to your codes imprinted
in fractions of mud, or up,
for that matter, to your commotions
calving new stars.

78

How long
and still entranced we are
by your surprises, we
believe you a body, perfect somehow
as a woman racked
with love, haloed by
her own heat, but offered, as it goes,
to any takers, you made
each brace of shadows twist
and shake.

Believing also
our bodies different
from yours, we were lost
in whatever thoughts
we robed you with. White
on the mountain, rivers the swish
of your tail, laughing harsh madame, free
with your earthquake favours, bellowing
death-songs we have sought
strange means to dominate you:
bridges, violins.

Naked
you might have appeared
to the old hunters. Should
I wear my shoes because
their masks and antlers,
fantastic forms invented
to contradict your moo, sprang into space
not without hope of wringing
from your bloody udder
drop by drop the pure milk.

In strawberry light
dances and sorcerers
rose from slime to outwit you.
Wise men watching the sea
chewed the lightning bolt. Cultures
built of their bones
crystallized
in tongues, in architectures, but

the great dome of imagined
destiny sat
capping the dreams that sweated
from spinal column and skull
our deadly chemicals.

Now, song, where
shall we go? No more to suppose
we can arrive at any
complete explanation; possibly
to live in truth apart
from paroxysms of the One; we have
a place in mind
offers the grip
to strip off not her hide
but the inedible crusts caking her,
their weight the imponderables
of history:
so like a moon her variety
sank, her wholeness
we instructed
in our oblivions, the clenched fist,
the frightened man's
mindless standard, death camp, swollen
the veins of orators convulsing
her whims into purpose.

Do not go back
to the swamp where, row on row,
the idols point. Rather to her,
at sixteen asking me
in the ice-cream parlour
how many dips, then dishing them out
with a flash of banded teeth. To someone
reading near dawn at some
ramshackle desk, aware
of the light reflected shaping itself
on a stone or piece
of an apple.

                    Go where I cannot,
                    anywhere the animals

are punished, with iron whips,
for our iniquities, and stop
voracity's fictions,
vengeance in its
continuous gathering
momentum, stop them
with a glimpse of her radiant
free
ongoing creation.

Also go to me,
who am answerable,
but walk a street through ruin
without so much
as the faint torchlight
of dejection.

OPOPONAX

A blue field for summer
Rib curve the dotted lines of lavender
Discontinuous flesh beating a signal out
And a man
Lifts a heart on his knife point
High

Possibly
He was hunting
He could be sacrificing
A squirt of cloud mixed in slow time
Would you believe it
With peace
It comes in a little bottle

In a little bottle
Knife in hand
A man stooped now he turns his terror
Like a fruit in the market
Palpitation of quanta
Like bomb bursts the line of lavender tufts

Now the tin cap sits tight
Rubber bung beneath
So the flashing knife will split
Memory down the middle
Mist of dawn on roofs multiform mask of cities
Moist chasm of spit and smells
Remembers the man

Now he strikes and again
But with five hundred baskets
Of flowers on its arms
Dew is calling out the names and prices
In a little bottle

Mountain throbs with rockfall
All its years at any moment
Distilled at a touch
On a fingertip fathoming the knife gash
Might balance or be crushed
Such crystal stars
Vast infolded systems
Index of man

Tenderness
And a great wet shroud
Catching the yellow blood of lavender

Extract the years of carnage
Touch your face

LE NU PROVENÇAL
(photograph by Willy Ronis, 1949)

The wooden shutter hanging open,
sunlight commands the shapes around the room.
A jug has left its ovals on a flagstone,
and tilts a little, as if listening in
to a kneecap or a buttock.
                    Not so the chair

82

with one leg out of touch with everything,
about six feet away across the floor.

If a round mat covers several flagstones,
what of the swirl of shadows all around,
tipping the chair, invading the towel that hangs
from the rail of an iron washstand, burrowing
into the armpit poised above the bowl.

The bowl is luminous enamel and contains
two hands, from one of which an arm sprouts
rounding into the gleam across a shoulder.
The mat, woven of rushes, also supports
the lines of feet mounting past the ankles
into calves that curve up into little pits
of light back of the knees.

                    Above the bowl
a mirror on a string, and where the frame
swooshes down to complete another oval,
a smudge of hair, a flit of shoulder show.

And the hair itself is tucked against a nape
never to be seen because the back's ellipse
conceals it, with a ripple of its flesh
and muscles held in tightly to the backbone.

Least mysterious of all a nipple charms
the bowl of white light with its bud, which echoes
across delicate dark waves of flesh
                         and is there again
in the round bottom and its dusky cleft.

Watch as you will, the mystery is elsewhere.
Perhaps between the things, distributing tensions.
Perhaps in the diagonals which cross, from chair
to shutter through the body, from the mirror
downward across the body to the jug.
Or in the volume of the space they occupy,
for such a little time sifting the silence,
buttressed at one end by the puckered wall
of stone and plaster, at the other end
by the gaze exploring all without distress.

THE POGROMS IN SEBASTOPOL

All night she wept,
Fania, ten
at the turn of the century,
this afternoon she saw
the tsar
in his karieta,

taking the curlers out
she had combed
her hair, long and blond,
she had washed her face, the tsar
waved
in his karieta
at everyone,

but in particular
the hand waves
cupped and white, feeling
its hollow through the hot
horse flanks,
inflexible dragoons,

at Fania freshly combed, noticing
her clean face, he waves
who is god-on-earth,
who for the good of his people
wishes
the Cossacks could make less noise
about it, a tidier business
next time,

and
besides
who waves his hand
at me, at me
all night she thinks,
weeping for joy, tsar, we say it
the same in Yiddish.

THIRD GENERATION

For two old immigrants
who do not speak the language
I drag this wooden dog
over the bending floor
of a corridor in their attic

It circles the town and crosses it
from one end to the other
many doors are swinging
open and shut as I pass
and the dog behind me clicketyclack

They lent me their plank
and played me the Mass in B minor
I lost the plank in a park somehow
or it turned into this dog
I am dragging for ever and ever

OLD WOMAN AT THE COUNTY DUMP

Sitting in her cracked hutch,
beneath trees, hidden from the road,
she is the guardian of a torrent
of burst mattresses, rust and rubber,
bodiless lids of objects without present function.

One tooth and a hank of hair,
a form of speech that spits and babbles
like the nerves of a scorpion in a jamjar.

Junk, mounds of it, from dark hollows
little dogs erupt, sniffing, stretch and disappear
like stars that fall in August. All the stuff
people have left, beyond and behind,
marching toward a world of absolute deodorants,
infallible laxatives.

What if she died?
Who'd notice? She might be found,
a few ribs and shanks, hardly smelling at all,
at home among the vacant basins. Her apocalypse
the O all these unbolted toilet lids
trumpet to the skies.

At night, I imagine,
stuck to her rocking chair, she dreams,
dreams of being guarded by the garbage.
A block of rusty bedsprings at her door,
plucked by rat claws, gives off
intermittent echoes of an old serenade.
With all its worms a portly wardrobe,
her protector.

I think of the lightning,
if it was lightning lashed from the waters,
the hiss of it, a sort of red
veined quaking cream, and frothed ashore
the whiff, a first, of space and time.

And I think of the women who floated
out of the forests, hard on the tracks of vague men,
thud of their feet, the wind's cry,
tall savannah grasses bending:
some carry in hollow logs
a yellow flame.

Puffs of smoke
struggle up from her heap of clapboard.
Still she is the guardian
of an element that signifies
a good roast crackling, a legend to live by,
of power tamed and change.

History
has beaten most of the life out of her body,
but still the days flash on,
nights blossom with new moons, the people
burst through time, breaking things like toys,
and leave her the rubble.

IDIOCY OF RURAL LIFE

for Kofi Awoonor

Where
begin: often it is
the disposition of objects
on a table:
        tall tin coffeepot,
blue saucepan, a membrane
of milk in it

Or: 'what a gulch,
Texas . . . .' the buzzard pecks
your politic racoons, gas
millionaires
        and smoke
machines horizon
the shadow of your smile

That
motel: fake pine panels,
over the interstice
        it is mulcted
Rainbo bread, a power
nails you: gaze
of a vacuumed stag head

Or: what finger might,
black or any, moonflower or toad,
make the infinite effort,
write 'Thy kingdom . . .' on the wall

Or: what voice
in a deep cavern echoed this
antlered dancer's rigmarole,
bucking and twirling;

        the void has drunk
bloodfoam, spun from the void, look,
a glittering web, spun by his dance measure . . .
my people have chosen

87

Dull demons:
first iron, then dynamite, painful
transformations, the peanut
gouged out of Africa, epochs like 1215,
1634, 1933
                         (Himalayan
tigers, what
new deceit, fanned by your breath, cooks
in the pot of spleen and okra)

Or: when electric
zeroes halt
the spate of babble, who shall decode
the alarm flushing from grass
goldfinch argosies,
                         palm leaves of Cumae,
who shall dance now
a sycamore in the wind

Or: the right verbs
here, and here, might relate
the things; then let these eyes
reap the sacred
space
between them

A WINDOW

Oddly like a porthole
It contains a thistle

Someone with a hammer fashioning stones
Imagined a deep square hole

And placed it in the wall it was real
Light in the morning returns to roost in it

No sea for a hundred miles
Among these unforsaken mountains
The deep square hole is white inside

And a hundred years afterward
Someone trod across the stone floor

Someone holding a vessel
Old glass and in it a thistle

Now the waves of light come crashing through
The blue head of the thistle

THE ULCINJ POSTCARDS

Truly, it takes the breath away,
This 'view',
The Adriatic, opal,
Unpopulated, and the dark now

Absorbing it. No wind,
Said Xristic, after sundown. The beach
Shrugs off its mass
Of splendid flesh—

What tentative hand
Carries along the sea wall, like lamps,
These young flat-bottomed women?
A major stomach, grandpaternal,

Does it shudder a bit when filling itself?
All the dusky shapes
Of appetition tangle, mask even
Such space as boys on tiptoe

Flit through. Had you
Lost the thread? Found, for *sladoled*, a table;
Two jugs; look up, the fort, 'attractive'
Turco-Venetian ruin;

And a tomb is built
Into a wall, hollow, candles 'twinkle'
At the foot of
A real coffin.

Godlike brigands, all gone; vestiges
Of their abrupt
Brilliance a mosque, the 'Chinese' house, and these
Nine heads on a rock, nine

White shirts, 'fierce moustaches'
Float in a shadow,
It hangs heavy, the last rock, one face
Gnawed to a slit by its own

Teeth: these be
Aboriginals—elsewhere
Hand in hand the families cluster,
Collectives trample, unemployed,

Up ankle-cracking alleys, chew the fragrant
Mutton, grilled on prongs,
And there is music. Behind a drainpipe
Tapping, too, is heard

At intervals, 'windless' intervals,
A tapping, strangest: the lizard
Busy in there, likely
Also a cricket

'Aims'
To be eaten, shucking off
Carapace and universe,
Twitch by twitch.

TRANSIT

Garden wall from this bed
Hollow square to support
                the faint harp sounds

In the acacia tree
                light flows and stays
It is filtering round arches
                            the gray spire

St. Germain from this bed of an early morning
It is an essence which breathes
                            or is savoured

An essence tasting of my entire time
My time clustering
                in the light which flows and stays

White curtain open window
                old harp to pluck
There are black cords
                        a palisade of cypress trees

My time passing them by as I wake
And hew down the cords
                one by one with a free hand

THE FOSSIL FISH

15 Micropoems
(Vaucluse: July—September 1969)

1

village quote idiot unquote
look a walking often takes
long at you

    stops & slow hows
    he come through

      screwy? clutched in
his one scrotum hand the other
crumpled hugs a fingering book

2

      them squads in
helmets
    burning
    the dragonfly's eyeballs
out
is just ants

3

   & silver eggs on stems
     be nobbut topknots
of a grass—ah savage head
   see them caught
       nodding in the wind launch your airy
hundredfold
   parabolas of seeing

4

          ivy around the capstone
             starts to fizz:
      early snailhorns are
            sounding the systems
     of their space

5

      shorts white
        at the sharp angle of
    trim bronze legs
         to a melon balanced
  in one palm she subtends her
       equilateral nose
           deepening the hidden
    rose of that sphere
        between cone & cone

6

  rock & bough
     tumbled over slammed against
pluck out their fillets
      of necessary flesh
   mad pleasure
  for once to bleed
      on a hill groaning
with apricot trees

7

inside the shell, fields:
        listen, lavender, wheat
    behind it, blue
            mountain behind
        the wheat, the sun
over the mountain, curving
    up, the wave murmur: it
        won't fall

                                8

                        storing its times
                        the body
                        learns weightlessness

                        space be skin
                        limit
                        my flesh of lightning

        9

    toad
    crawls
    up
    boulders
    always
    dragging
    his
    ughs!

10

                    a place ribbed with quartz between
                        soaring
                            rock wings here the wind
            swivels crashing sucked
                                back into its helix
                luminous flesh in which
                    embedded far below beyond
                        float mountains little
            mossy tuffets

11

feeling the leaf
a tree
wrote
spine
longwise it is not
chinese but crinkles

12

            calm in the face of nature

            fearful in the face of nature

            maggot, neither, holes
                up in a peach

13

to please a nymph
     sip at her spring
so her true voice told
     first a far cry
now sharper breaths
     moisten this rosy moss
& soon for sure
     she will be coming

14

coming also his long gusts tell me
the wind a river he roars
     in pine trees pounding walls of rock
to destroy he scatters to build

speech a silver breath & seed once he scooped
     a whole man from a cave
     flicked him away
like an eyeball

     with twisted clay
trumpets at dawn we call for him hopeless
     on the mountain

he floats in the crested ocean eastward
     blue cattle waiting to drink
the first torrent of rays

     how else from his flowering
chiselled hollows
     could these bee snouts tap our honey

15

the fossil fish
hides in time
for now it is the season

& all the hunters come
with long clean rifles

UNTITLED

When you got up at four to make pipi,
I walked to the window & pushed open the shutters.
Silver crescent moon in a sky of clear dark peach colour.
One star a thumb's length from it shot from the bow.

There was a silence, the kind you can hardly remember.
You came back to bed & I was in beside you.
To touch your breast was all a new day,
Warm & cool your legs were hitched around my waist.

Beginning slowly it is a violence creates mountains.
Now a moon & a star stand over the ridge quietly.
Here in this little mound between your legs I touch you;
So a star could begin to appear in another person's eyes.

Of that violence we make what we tenderly do,
Rock & moan, laugh & weep for the joy of it;
But the window is open, swallows tweet dotted quavers & cut
                                                        loose.
As the rooster calls I count the heads that will roll today.

CHANEL ALWAYS NOW

for Friederike Mayröcker & Ernst Jandl

1

by sir francis rose
      a combination of sheer poetic lust
  hard work
and important artistic was fifteen. she had come
      like a slim youth.
          then when she moved
  a small dark boat on water.

2

    striped sails Chanel
but small and fascinating. flat figure
and great-smallness was at all costs. must reveal.
    fragile greek faience mask
    lying in a miniature nest of sawdust.

3

    coins on cotton wool
in a small white tortoiseshell
    which he would twist around his neck several times
  it hung
heavily down to a pocket
    in his trousers. the goddess
  of mentally women
      and a woman of boni de castellane covered all
her large square sofas.
    poiret and bakst
the palely powdered women in their forties.

4

Chanel destroyed this very expensive boyish
little girls of the working class.
buses and aeroplanes.
boyish line of the sports field and english
public school
luxury except in the details. heads bare and sleek.
valentino
brilliantine hats were bullets. very solid.

5

kit wood who died admired
the great ivory negro nancy wore on her arms
but not the junk Chanel made fashion
for the first time.
hide bare skin up
to the shoulder. a pendant bosom
made for lady abdy toussaint a large blue
egyptian in gold lotuses
like a miniature temple.

6

much was simple. it was opposite.
it was essentially. nothing could have been.
she made that. taste abominable. square.
scent bottles. everything Chanel. black walls.
black *toile ciré*. kitchen tables. don antonio de gandarillas.

covering paris the power of the scottish mackintosh.
I forced my mother with shoulder straps.
it was one of the mysterious objects I have seen.

blue cape
in the french navy another time
labourers' gauntlets of coarse hide
dyed a pale sky blue
on the palms. now called pop. inspired.
shanghai blues by all the pimps
these cotton chinese colours
not forgotten.

peter blarney the greatest doyenne of proust in 1930
said: I adore her for the italian stitching the madwoman
of costume. jo dufy said: Chanel makes rounded horses.
andré hemingway said: I do not understand without sex
for literature in dressmaking. dolly sister jennings
said: they have always said

black velvet
but my fox terrier loved the chinchilla
so I made it into his bed. boni de cocteau
the most extravagant man said:
*la femme fait la cuisine avec les garçons de Chanel mais
c'est la bonne cuisine d'une paysanne.* thank god
in 1926: the machine lace
is far more important than clothes.

scot bibesco the russian virgil gertrude tchelichev
alice b lavery jean-gabriel serge and lifar thompson
said:

le tout paris are dreams
      a woman with a face
       an outline
         goes to your concerts
           she has destroyed beautiful hats
              magical creature

coco

      Chanel a lovely dress one forgets it
   with going up to bed Chanel is politics
  after all Chanel stripped women
a date palm without dates Chanel

     her head a little boy in black tights
      for a masque by inigo jones
       a monument of palm leaves
      at the end of the party
this wonderful headdress

    I lost it in a gust of wind on the way home

(Collage from a text by Sir Francis Rose, in *American Vogue*
December 1969)

NINE BIPLANES

for Ricardo Gullón

una vaga astronomía
de pistolas inconcretas
(Federico García Lorca)

Summer 1940: I opened the double glass front door of that rambling country mansion, school, and saw nine biplanes flying low, in close formation, and slowly; the lower edge of what I saw is a ruffled green mass of trees.

But I do not know what day it was, or the month, only that the summer had begun. And there may have been six biplanes, or twelve. Certainly they were biplanes, heavy ones, with two motors, and they were moving slowly, as if a great wind belaboured them, though the trees were hardly moving, there was no wind, or just a little. I opened the front door, was standing on the gravel path which looped a large flower bed, and then came the noise.

Now, looking out of the window, I see a low wall of rocks, a section of gray drainpipe stood on end as the base for a bird feeder, a green bush, and behind these, somewhat higher, a mass of foliage, and behind the foliage a sky, frameless, though parcelled into infinity by bird calls delineating territories, and beyond that, the real sky. A child looking the same way sees deep down, a window, and deeper, little pine tree, clear lake, another window, and deeper, little pine tree, its image, in a clear lake.

The noise is still loud and clear. Looking upward I saw the biplanes. I had heard about the war, but nobody had said much about it, except, now, that the Germans had broken through. They said it, yet one saw nothing; at any moment, they said, it might happen, the invasion. They, whoever they were, spoke of invasion, invasion, and there we were, eating toast, miles from home, running up and down the long corridors, and doing extra Latin. The schoolmaster went on smoking his pipe, whacking us with his slipper, and writing neat equations with his goldnibbed Onoto pen. It was an odd thing, so much noise, overhead, and rushing out of the house, more than a house, a country mansion, after crossing the immense panelled hall, and opening the door, and now to be standing there on the gravel, looking up, and seeing the biplanes.

Nine or six biplanes, already oldfashioned, as one knew from pictures in the papers, flying somewhere, to fight, in the sky, somehow, the Germans, who had broken through.

Deeper still, a street in Hué or An Loc, no, this time Barcelona, and a little girl's head being sliced off by a bomb splinter, her mother clutching at the body, two soldiers in bedraggled uniforms looking at the head, down at the head, which lay at their feet.

They were flying across Norfolk, toward the sea perhaps. Woods, the breckland, miles of wheatfields and dark barns, heading toward the sea. The Germans were not at sea at all. What were they looking for? How would they identify it when they found it? They had been told to fly. So they flew, airmen, wearing leather helmets, which are not blown off their heads because of the leather straps and the buckles. Signals from their home base filling the cockpits, determined looks on their goggled faces, the air humming among the wires we drew crisscross between the two wings when we made our sketches.

When people are blocking the French road, exploding steel mouths gobble their canaries, grandparents, and bolsters. Deep down, a clear lake, it reflects the sign to be seen in a certain Moscow elevator in 1937: It is prohibited to put books down the lavatory.

They sat in the cockpits, looking determined, with orders to fight the Germans, if they found them, knowing that their machines were rickety and ridiculous. Maximum speed 150 m.p.h. Down there on the gravel I heard the droning clatter of their motors. Type of armament: unknown. Range: uncertain.

Seeing German soldiers marching into the Saarland, they were marching on the front page of the *Daily Sketch*, made me ask one day in the basement kitchen, with the paper spread out before me on the kitchen table among jampots and knives and cups: So is there going to be a war? My mother at the stove, without turning around to face me, must have said Yes or No, probably No; but with the biplanes flying in close formation low overhead, I was not remembering this.

The men wearing helmets and sitting in the cockpits of the old biplanes were not twiddling their thumbs or drinking pop, but they were English. Perhaps they knew about the bombing in Spain, whereas I knew nothing, or had noticed nothing, except the Crystal Palace Fire, the Abdication, the faraway deep throbbing at sea through late summer nights, before September, when German armies marched into Poland, and Polish cavalry with sabres launched attacks on tanks, I knew nothing about bombing in Spain but thought I must have heard fleets of submarines moving out into the Atlantic. So these airmen were setting out, on a summer's day in the fifteenth century, to fight the enemy, flying low, in close formation, and I had rushed through the panelled hall, had opened the door, and now stood and stared at them, my feet on the gravel, my head tilted back, mouth open, and did not realize that this was what was happening. A loud noise in the sky, continuous. Antique gesture.

A child, instead of looking downward, now looks outward, and still cannot awake, the inability to awake being, like an arm's reach or the tilting of a head, part of his condition. With hacked-off hands he constructs for himself someone else, old, scribbling. Amid the droning clatter of the motors, a bell of pink fire suddenly sounds. He listens to the long trumpet blaring tightly across the neolithic heath, on which he found flints during Sunday afternoons; he listens to the flying metal blare and does not see the girl's head rolling across the gravel to his toecaps.

The sounds are people running in plimsolls, knock of the red leather ball on the willow cricket bat. A smell of linseed oil in the thatched pavilion. But the pilot's head is wrapped in leather: the pilots are going to knock the Germans for six, if they can find them, behind the pavilion, between the pavilion and the woods, where you could hear the cock pheasant scream before any thunderstorm, or, in the evening twilight, quietly see rabbits feeding, their ears laid back along their little skulls.

FRACTIONS FOR ANOTHER TELEMACHUS

1

Clutching the oars he sweeps the small blue wave across a sea of
colours. Deep and blue, with wefts of sand across shallows;
green, or crowded with fish, or speckled with islands, flesh of
pineapples, many-chambered. Nights and days, cities fume on
the coast, there are prairies, there are lagoons

2

Horse from his field
Hoof by hoof uncurling
Up he stands
Tidy

With pink lips
A cow has plucked a leaf
Soft
Chafing the cherry tree

Tongue and a gust of air
Comb the golden horse tail
Flying

3

While he rows the wave, she sits facing him, holding the
rudder. Sometimes she is leaning back, the wave speeds
forward and her hair, long and dark, flows out over the wake.
His cry, most ancient shriek of shepherds and of sorcerers, high
pitched, holding to the bloodiest red edge of agony, with
laughter, carves out of the space before them the shapes of
action, halcyon wings, the spread of trees

4

Nature what is this joy
Your strain to the heart

Reek of a crocodile swamp
The solitary pihi
Pecking freshest horse apples

Is it good like bread and simple

A rotting goddess
Torn by the hair through times unthinkable
Tells me nothing

The little girl knows it
In a shadow she has curled
Anxious fingers
Around her sea shell

Her donkey
And funny human feet
At the end of the garden
Wild often spinning in the dance

Birds desperate almost hurry
Their song

Or her hair may be silvery gold and tight curls. Times come
when she lowers her hood and hides her face; or she spreads her
knees but lets the rudder go. Then she throws back the hood, in
a fury, her face is tilted upward, eyes widening hack through
clouds, there is a purple space and she wrestles with it, her
cheeks like wax, her white robe fluttering, the rest of her a
death, so still, except for the tears that are streaming into the
folds around her throat

Now this lion is full of blood
Looking into the shotgun barrels

Even in my sleep they are pointing at me
Patient

Don't shoot crumpety janitor
Your steel food freezes me mouth upward
I gulp the treasure air
Speak

And afterward
The diamond snake has ringed the whole earth
Hold on to your head
Listen

Listen as he sniffs the little white horns
Upside down
Out of the rain the opening rain flowers

7

And when she is laughing he answers . . . *parthenikoi* . . .
haliporphuros . . . *hieros ornis*—words he never heard in
Macedonia. His people, they love him seldom, and they do not
know whether he speaks of meat or of time. They may come at
him with diagrams, with calendars, with pictures. He leaves
them with a sign, only a sign, which has no weight; and when
they throw away the sign it stays in mid-air, perceptible only as
a measured pulse, coming and going, as an ache or a whiff of
pinewood, unplaceable. If the strongmen see the wave
approaching, they run to the shore, stand on their heads, and
shout, kicking with their booted feet: Death to the betrayer of
all first things

Side by side
How close our bodies and we walk
Down the long gun barrel

Asleep in the lion's darkness
In the scattered features of these people
The torrent of flesh storming toward me
Find your face I never could find

Your face

So she goes, the village girl
Nada Nada
Once too often whipped
By her mother

Down the hill a steep
Track and up she is
Plunging into the gorge
Definite orphan going no place

And around I go in a glistening rose
The one wave will gather me and scatter
Moonlight solid salt
Crunch me Nada
The trumpet blare of bitter grasses

First a clear long horizon
Show me the aureole now she says
Three far peaks and the aureole over them
A sky of skin never touching for tenderness
Remote remote

(*Explicit* Victor Boris Shklovsky: 'There is a time which is substitutive
and interrupting, a sporadic time: the time of the voyage of
Telemachus.')

AVOCADO PLANT

How good it was
to burst from the nut
now my roots dangle in clear water

white roots trailing gripped by little turrets
cockfeather cloud I plant in ears
a sting of wind

yet nothing shakes me from the split
nut held in the mouth of the bottle
and my sixteen leaves shot from the tendril

quilts pointed at either end
and oval
only hatch these tufts of shadow

flicked across the wall as I climb forever
out of myself on the sunbaked zinc
casing of an old water-fan

A DRIVE IN THE COUNTRY /
HENRI TOULOUSE-LAUTREC

Drawn out of the bones of light,
Definite figures, a few, ordinary.

As if in its bones the light had known them,
All: the horse, trotting away,
The yellow trap, and in their Sunday hats
Face to face, the man and the woman.

Properly, half a man and half a woman.
Come to that, only half a horse.
Locomotion, yet essential muscles
Are hidden in the picture; even the dog,

Athwart, running behind the yellow trap
Like the wind—not a leg in sight.

Gone any moment,
Beautiful creaking old trap drawn by half a horse.
No, not that. It is the way
A definite hat plume centers everything
On a still point in the sky.

Or the hatcrowns compose
One imaginary diagonal streaking off
Into the sky's oblong blue; and it is nice,
The way it slants against the lower
Green diagonal of the field's edge.

Not even that. The dog—great cool gush
Of the air across his nostrils. Not that:
Shot with rose, an undulation of shadow
Racing the trap, a feather's cusp,
Magnified, as dog, and sideleaping
Not from a hat but from the road.

Not so, not so; a presence, tacit,
Holds in place, for the eye to strike them,
Fugitive signs in their consortium: an egg!

Interior oval, its yolk,
A yellow trap, the crystal sun chariot—
Across the emerald cone, an egg, tilted,
That is what the figures make and are made of.

Parabola, it begins
At the tip of the horse's ears, it hugs
The hatcrowns, rounds the dog's tail,
Returns to base along the curve from wheel to hoof.

Even then, not so.
It never was an egg. If not, what else,
What else but the eye of Henri Toulouse-Lautrec:

And hiding it had spied
Upon itself, slicing itself
In half, had scooped up this other universe
Out of the escaping bloody mucus; now
The figures dwelling in it,

Healed, flawless, are the very nerve
That sees, and they retreat from you
Because of this,
When all the time it happens to be there.

ANASPHERE: LE TORSE ANTIQUE

> *kami naraba*
> *yurara-sarara-to*
> *ori-tamae!*

I

Among the grains how small you were
Dry in the desert of your image

You did not hear the cries of love as you passed
Down the street, you did not see
The spittle
Fly nor the beads of blood on the axe blade

The naked masked woman
Twice she swung it & once more & high
By its long handle

II

Here we are travelling from place to place

Here I keep you hidden
Held by a great lightness
Body & voice if I could set you free

In my cage a castle rose to its turrets
Only for mice & a flock of ravens
Pure columns unbent by thought

111

Here they shall flower from our stillness
Voice their future dream
Of being trees

Plant them giving shade in a field
For five cows composing a sign for us
The diagonals of a dice
Or it is the pentagram—
Hidden in a bed the conversation of bodies
Hidden I keep them

And still there is a voice
Whenever in sweet nakedness you nuzzle me
Voice I want you not only to say

A white cow is made of cream & fury

—Hathor

So your face took shape
It was in the boulders uphill before us
A movement of lines to the measure of a dance
A flashing of earth years Egyptian axes and eyes
No time at all in which it happens

One hundred thousand horses
Toppling off the crag were chopped into food
For the hands that peeled leaves of laurel
Out of the flint core
Now in a field of old rain goofily like a fortress
A red horse was planting his hooves
—Look how it is to stand there

Devastation
Marks no tracks of ours
Lightly now through these hidden places we shall walk
Where mouths collect & change to make expressions
Listen
A street with many twistings this one

Lightly you are here you had no weight whatever
Wearing your little cloak over so much nakedness
You leaned against me

III

1

Body of light
      Dwelling in a piss jet
Or particular cherry blossom

       Look, a spirit
Wanted something
      A sign, to be manifest
          In all directions

   Never
Sure, inhaling itself
        A whirlwind

2

      Desire, pressing
On silence
   To lure you, poem
One or two words

   Go
To the southern shore
        One flesh we pursue

3

      One, through Never—
A span, slightest across
        Perdition, horrible
   Deep, the gurgle

It is
Pepper behind my eyes, it fashions
The eye of the hurricane
It fills
With snakes & stars
The liquid cathedral collapsing across
Atolls, Florida keys

4

World, great harp
Built of blood
Now then
What sounds in flight

What muscular forms of breath
Never flow, leap
Up the torrent & restore

To you
Your open tunes

5

One flesh—
Other, another
Horizon, ancient
Unplaceable

Twitter your speech again
Models
Out of oblivion
The bud & the wave & the snowflake

6

Your never is yes,
Out of nowhere the cry
Gone & again
Cupola, welling, spiral, it lifts from

The bird throat

Soon hushed

But song in
Some few broken
Tombs

A touched sex

IV

Difficult
Piecing the life together

'like a supper in the wind'
How it comes, goes
Exact from perception
Rhythm

Not snatching
It comes in waves
Not knowing me from you
A spirit cannot be spoken
Or spoken of

Drums drumming the exact measure
Dancer to dancer the flower spray is passed

To build for you a space
    In this drain of being it is I
   Smash the heads & fix famine
A floor strewn with rock-orchid
                   Lotus roof

In mid-air, air dangerous with heat
      Carbonic gas, beams of cassia
I have suspended
   A floorspread weighted down with white jades

Margins, like these
     Then at sun up to have leapt into
The blue fragrant living sea

Profit motive melts the poles
       Paris drowning, Bombay
Alexandria

I have hung strips of flesh at porch & gate
    The flesh of children

The time will not come again
           It will not come again

Note: the epigraph, from the twelfth-century Japanese text *Ryojin Hissho*, means: 'If you are a god,/With a swing and a swish/Deign to come down.' See Arthur Waley, *The Nine Songs* (London 1955, p. 14), source for certain ancient Chinese shamanic motifs in sections III and IV.

GINESTRA

What on earth makes it possible—
Over rocky slopes
Yellow explodes and replenishes itself,
With pulse on pulse an airy
Marine perfume floats and is
A robe of shivers around the mountain

It must be contained
In the chemical roots
Nothing explodes, the yellow simply
Unfolds; nothing,
Nevertheless, unfolds like this,
Metaphor and fact refuse to mix

And the plant hangs in such
Delicate balance the wonder is
Yellow shrank in us to a blazon
For jealousy. Here no
Body of self or doubt or fury bends desire,
Bolts a door or kicks it in

These great birds fly
Full stretch in their perfume,
Their talons fit the quartzy
Generous ground,
And in the slant

Light as night came, in sips
Of yellow pastis we drink them down,
Slow, all but
Rippling in the broom as in bamboo
One diligent Chinaman, long ago

IN THE SECRET HOUSE

for Ann

Why lean over the fire, and who is this
Being
Vaguely human, who
Watches the steam float from wet boots
And regards the rose interiors

Various woods keep
Recomposing themselves; nothing holds
In the fire, the fire is always
Less than it was, the fire—

Expulsion
Of old smells, new intangible horizons
Does not hear through its decay,
Calling in the cold
Rain, the little owl, one note
Over and over

Nor, under its breath, does the fire give
A thought to the petrified
Print of a snail, its broken wheel—
Rays on a rock at the hearth's edge. Who
Is this, and who thinks

Through the fire, sees the rayed shell,
Solid axis, the whirling death
Of some incorrigible small thing
Before the ice came

Before the ice came carving out the mountain
And the fire took
Or took care of someone
And the house was constructed
In a cloud of goats, coming, going,
Before the cockerels

Put down their tracks, cry and claw,
Through generations, this fly
Settled on the breadloaf—

So stare, into the fire, and what for
The important
Citadel, towers of light, crepuscular
Tunnels, simply face
The black rain, blue wave
Of mountain birdsong

Mud on my hands, little owl, it is
No grief to share with you,
Little owl,
The one note, not lost, for nothing

CELESTE

looks like them elementals just poured
a glass of blue champagne
and you look up
—silver fizz—
because your body
is
the stem

DISCOURSE ON LEGEND

I hug to my breast
The green head of wheat
And I suckle it
          Forough Farrokhzad

Legend, you are the one, the who
The woman jumping out of the global box
The song the wave the blue in the veins
Which has no completion

Try as I may to decipher you
I find no text at all
When I riffle the book to find a rule
You escape, happily
Cleaning your teeth with a carrot;
Or a certain African king, for him
As you knot your hair and strip,
I hear you cough, ahem, in a vast
Green Sahara of hope and desire

Or you have cut the world's
Irascible droning
Throat and wallow, legend, you,
In the blood. You give yourself
To the hilt, yet
Every drop,
Your own undulant
Body drinks it back, freely the torrent
Returns, and you, legend,
Swing through the maze with never a blank
Drawn, from pulse to pulse. Speak

And you rip heads off
The cardboard
Categorizing men who try
To read you. Laugh

And you speak a song, I hear it
Far off as the wind
Sucks and guzzles
A single grain of sand and whips
The flesh of moons
Wicked habit tramples. Legend,

Do not be deceived
By the mechanical gesture,
Yours or any. Do not think
That you repeat yourself
To death.
You'll die more easily, with a croak
In a goatskin tent, in Italy a cough,
A flash of your laugh
May extinguish you
On a ship, but not this, not

You, anonymous,
Crosseyed
Kissing your knee, not
For fascination fingering your bush
All curled up in a madhouse.

But
But I could be wrong
I could be wrong, and when or where
It starts, the track of this
Incomprehension, I alone (this
I whom you
Provoked and
Must ignore) can ask. Of what? Ecoute,
O godforsaken oracle, écoute . . .

If it is in
A certain falsity, which bends all sense
When thought like twilight
Spirals up from its depth to meet
A promise of connection, legend, is it you

Multiplies and snarls the track,
Do all the flying
Jagged particles
Connect
By grafts drawn from the dark
Body of legend?

You, distinct, and
No other, but
Escaping
Autodestruct, so
Like a civilization bent on death
You might be a messenger, come
From the core of life with his tongue cut out,
Or a mirror
In the pure
Instant as it falls
To the stone floor, and

From the impact, shattering, has
Already arisen the wand of mimosa,
Yellow, without
Fracture, stillness in a room,
A melon is glad to be round like that,
Lips parting, listen, the first
Sound
Of a speech for an exchange
Of natures
Between things and people, a joy arises also
Giving this blue to the sea,
To the city its dawns and sacred statues

And in some, legend, among us
A spirit responds, not
So as to speak of it, with a longing
To be
Reborn.

CAROMB, VAUCLUSE

For the giant boy who plays
Alone
Pétanque in a yard

For the idiot girl
Who sings at the wrong time
Stone feet
Plunged in a dance of fish

For the white & yelping
Imbecile afloat
In the same old stream

Listen to the shriek
It is only the hirondelle

This rush of wings

Listen to the fly, it is not a fly
The buzz of weight
Is fattening a fig

Which you peel, as is right
They say
Never peel a peach
You need not fear

This blue tint on a vine leaf
The shivering part
Of sunrise

A DARK LINE

Far off, a beach, the sea
Blue heat lives
In the sand, but far off
Real sea and she swims in it
The girl with Moroccan
Mysterious hair

Swims the long distances
A dark line traversing day discovers
Itself in her body
Swimming

Breath comes and goes
Body sheathed in cool salt
Separation and closure
Of the breasts as her arms
Have spread and again
She folds them

The long distances almost forever
Forgotten beach, the same talk
Over and over, swept toward
Unspeakable stars

By the arms and legs
By the breath going out and in
And out—
Spread on the sea floor far
Under her, far

An ancient ship
Crusts of shell and a coin or two
Beams half buried
Cargo of squid in figured jars
An old prow pulling
Once in a while
Like a curtain of moonlight
The depth aside

NIGHT BLOOMING CEREUS

The student has woolly hair
& a clear mind. He
is intent, he explains

the poem's genesis. In
certain terms,
a boot

being a boot, here
is deixis, there anaphora,
deleted

the entire predicate, glow
came to substitute
for green, & who

wrote it, someone? In a
hazel bush? Now suppose
you 'unexpress the expressible,'

these two parts
of speech, at random juxtaposed
make (something)

(new) having
begun with, or not, but what
was the link

it is jolly, a morning
fog overnight devastated Austria,
clunk

of (pause) (deletion)
noun on (overmuch
consonance). Here the pen

scratches 'relation,' 'procedure,'
you have to feel it,
bones in the hand

remember a walk
uphill—battered cemetery—
the little one, lonely, a hand, the

notion of being
'fathered', born, that is, first off,
then to find

a warm solid through the blur,
company ('helpless'),
so what is it

imagination, a
factory, grinding out, like
sentences, one by one,

ghost forms, they hover
back of each
(substitution) construct

we select, for instance,
filter & select
a basis, become competent

(variable, to be sure)
& identify
a scream, a star, this 'political'

system, that
vestige of a bird
in a woman. He did not,

someone, he did not
want it so, an
overwhelming otherness planted

'boundless space
in a square foot of
paper,' the work on words

begun, it was
a fragrance, dank, filling
the courtyard, then the laugh

a wind popped in his body
shells
of seed sounds, an alternative

universe is
composing itself in slow measure, not
as in Manhattan

walk, rapt, & listen
to the fire bells, repeat, fire
bells around the clock, but

these cups
of nameless flowers
had opened, once

only, white, a few hours
& heady
through the night, inside them

forty fifty filaments
drip
from tiny golden knobs pollen,

out it thrusts
from below that annual cupped mass
the pistil, a trumpet

split-mouthed, open, star,
avid this
reaches out, not a breath, all

insides, into the night,
& moistens
for something, something, promise

to the last drop. Now the moth,
fresh-hatched,
has to come to it.

SNAIL ON THE DOORSTEP

Snail on the doorstep
Is it rain or dusk
Plants giving off odour of sheep's fleece
So strong the curls cling
Wet between fingers

Snail on a doorstep far south
A radio knob you want to turn it
(Knees crack as you crouch to see it)
For news and think another catastrophe
News counts the decay
And substance of sacred things

Snail on the doorstep knees cracking
Light from nowhere
Point like a pyramid strikes the shell
Strikes the ultimate
Spiral centre

It is this expanse only an expanding
Centre of the spiral
The light stops where it started
But the snail on the doorstep
Uncoils in the light and blooms

The pyramid whispering expands
It follows the infinite curve of space
It ends where it started
If this were not a snail
There could be no universe

If this were not a snail
Another door would not let out
These children
They would not have crept
Under the mulberry on tiptoe
Fingers to their lips

All the snails would roll
Hightailing it away from them
Startled horns aswish to test
Cooler air
Not spirals like the sun

A SMALL BRONZE OF LICINIUS I

His beard, clipped trim, looks like
A chin strap, but
Is broader, he meant it
To clamp for ever to his skull
The wreath of three spikes. Sixteen years
A small but stylish emperor—

This round eye gazed out, at home
Inside a circle
And the circle was made of letters
Telling the world his titles and his name.
Toga folds were clasped below
By a ring
Where neck joined shoulder

Ready to stab or sing
The spikes
An open beak with a tongue stuck out—

Not so the sportive
Actual profile, nose to nose
With the immediate, for flesh is total,
Power the rage, you bend
Every nerve on timing
Countertricks—Fortuna shifts
Her weight, another
Fist
Slugs flat the monstrous glory. When

When if ever did the true
Eye detect
The head of Constantine? Constantine
Pushed with his palm
Coins across the table, worn
Stockpiled silver, harvests of bronze
Mint as this one

And the troops of Constantine took
Such coins by the handful
And bit them, with Turkish yellow
Dog teeth hopefully
They bit them

HEARING ELGAR AGAIN

for D. M. M. at 75

Not crocked exactly, but in a doze,
There I was, before supper time: Elgar,
Stop your meteoric noise, the glory
Leaves me cold; then it was
I woke to the melody—

Back, a place, 1939, and people
Singing, little me among them,
Fresh from a holiday
Summer, beside the Cornish sea, I sang
In chorus with a hundred English people.

You choose to live, as far as possible,
Spontaneously. So life is all
A wandering—curious orchestra, the whole
Sound of it accords with such
Invention of melody, song half-buried

By tympani, trombones, the glorious hot
Imperium. A life proceeds,
It is all, all of it, found in the instant:
Look, flowing, a friend shone, but wizards,
Drunken, forgot what I have to say

And underneath, in her garlic subway,
Busbied Persephone stands and waves
Her tambourine, a rabbit
Drums little feet on a village green, the snare
A moon halo strangling him.

Mother—we have gone on while others,
We remember, flew as ash into the sky.
To what? We have gone
On, dense trees, birdsong in cool petals
Never the ignored sustenance;

Rolling music is what deceives us, only
An appetite springs from the core,—
Melody, in a flash,
A harsh frog croaks in the creek now,
A bit of rain has touched my hand. Why?

POLLEN

1

Sweet & bitter & unsolicited
The smell
Drifting up from inside my shirt
All of a sudden
Fresh cut pine log

131

2

Tug at the tangled string
I think
Therefore I draw this up

Steep roofs collecting snow
Perhaps Ratzeburg, the lake ice
Immense on a road
Broken back of a Holstein stallion

3

Alles kaputt. In 1946
Kartoffelschnapps. Loot:
A bellyful of turnip. Sludge caked
The Humber's axle when we clambered out
Hunting dynamos,
Parachutes, invisible nazis

4

Now southwestern daylight streams
Into an empty
Teacup, it has me
By the hairs, fresh cut log,
Pine log

5

Squadron Leader Butt blanketed in
Sheepskin
Barges through the door, with a shout
Scaring the guard shitless:
'I come from Vladivostock!'

6

Mexican buckeye forks
From stony ground, red flowers
Of the wild thyme
Nod across the interface, with bees,
They break nothing nohow

Tiny Butt I ask you
What are we to do with them
If we find the nazis

Now it's howdy

7

These winds
They bring you almost
Anywhere you never meant to go

THE PROSE OF WALKING BACK TO CHINA

The poem began when I walked out,
Early, discovering forty minutes to go
Before the traffic would raise its roar.
It was nothing at all but the motion
Of walking, nothing at all
But the sight of a fish head in a heap
Of trash in a pail, a flower, an egg shell,
Until I began to compose it in my head.
And until
An amazed man with a beard scooped
Colour photos out of a cardboard box
Close to a wall, and a couple of doors away
A dog discovered a bone in a bin,

My skin thickened. A mouldy lemon
Took the first heat of day in the Rue Madame
As I turned to the left
And an old lady
Hosing the pavement said: 'Il faut
Arroser, hein?' with a laugh, and I
Actually found the words to say: 'La rosée même,
Madame, c'est vous.'
Was this the poem? Up Rue Vavin it went,
With shirts in a window, was
It this, the stacks of little magnetic cakes
In the patisserie where schoolgirls go,
And this, in La Rotonde, the waiter of
Two years ago not recognizing me?
The trash truck whines as it grinds
Rot to powder; the poem
Attacked by fleets of random objects
Had no purity or perspective whatever.
Ninety tomorrow Marc Chagall declares
You are nothing if you have
Materialist ideas. A capless man
Sponges down the glass walls of the bus shelter.
Again I scan the print, see: Nuclear reactors,
Negociations, a charge of treason,
Crucial support, failed to progress,
Emigrate to Israel, why do the words
Come in the plodding rhythm of the poem
If the poem isn't? Now the sun's heat
Goes up another notch, I gulp
The last of the coffee and trundle on,
Along the Boulevard Montparnasse,
Crisscrossing it
For a line of books, a cluster of lamps,
A Syrian store with distinctive
Waistcoats, coral and silver on display,
Suddenly arrive, walking the poem,
There where the chestnut trees in full leaf
Frame lawns punctuated by statues.
The sprinkler's long horizontal bar
Rotating flung the water up in a fan,
So that it fell
Far across the grass and over the wavering

134

Fronds (at least I thought
These were 'fronds'), it dripped from the beards
Of bronze lions topping the pedestal
Of an old lamp, this might be
A thing to watch, like the poem
You can't write, ever, this
Machine dispensed
Freshness, beginning
Everywhere it touched, for sparrows
And the grass at least. I
Sat in the sun which had risen
Above the long green wave
Of Indistinguishable Trees, in the dust
My boots were settling among
Delicate prints of the feet of birds,
A broken egg shell, also a naked
Razor blade. The blackbird
Is listening for a Worm, he
Can place it by a slight
Shift of his head, and I was listening
For the poem, but heard, placeable nowhere,
Pure low Bach notes on a flute,
The flute
Undulates, the dove's flight
Undulates, descending spray
Fans out like nervous wings from shoulder blades
And floats to earth as the flute again
Soars upward. A dog trotted across
The sunlit opposite street. A gnat
Glittered for an instant in mid-air.
From where I am the flute is clear,
I cross the grass to be closer, it has gone,
Almost, into the traffic's roar.
A woman in an open window says
'Yes, I hear it, sometimes, yes,
But I don't know, I live here, yes,
But really I don't know,' and on she went
With the ironing. Could she be
A scalded grandchild of one of those women
The musician took through a secret door
In Saint-Merry? Not for bewitching as
Her grandma had been? The flute

Plays on and on and I thought
Not the moon is seen but fingers pointing,
How could she ever tell me
What can't be matched by dharma?
Perspective makes a space intelligible,
But you only find the place to stand
By moving as you may, for luck, so nothing,
Nothing in the voice
Guides the poem but a wave
Continually broken,
And restored in a time to be perceived,
As the flute is perceived, at origin,
Before creation.

SALAMI IN ROMANSHORN

That salami in Romanshorn, so
good the taste of it, so
good,
a slice, the first, another, & the bread
white, not too much

donkey
gristle, nor smoke, a piece
of the best, a cut, she said, above
the human,
& set down the book, not

the greatest, right
there, opposite
the salami, so the book shall do some
eating too, no, I mean
be like it, kind of

admire the salami, maybe
read some. Where
was this? On the beach? Other stuff
going on
around the world? Lots, but shoot, if

anything mattered,
aside from
that salami &
the book, anything, sure why not,
she'd like to know of it

THE WINTER POPLARS

seventeen
in a line, outside
your window, widen your eyes, but
still are shut, one by one, tight shut

ghosts
          upspring
                        imagine
the first touch
of green, an alteration of smells, how it is
to wear a long leaf dress

what lightness
to grow from your good eyes
inward
a substance of bone & dream
                                        out there
only what can be seen begins

but living is, & is, one of a kind,
faith, which makes
actual what should be there,
                        felt on your pulse
the full tree, fluttering

it does the world
out of a death, for nothing then,
nothing can take hold of you

OR ELSE

As I went into the tabac to buy two boxes of matches, I happened to glance to my right. Or else, as I glanced to the right on going into the tabac to buy two boxes of matches, or else I had gone into a tabac to buy two boxes of matches, and glancing to the right I saw a small woman, not old, not young, perched on a chair, and she was eating what I took to be a tartine, or else the remnant of a tartine. She held the bread in both hands, like a squirrel, and her feet did not touch the floor. She was a very small person, and her face was round and white.

Then I asked for the matches, paid for them, and while turning to leave took a second look at the small woman. It was a small tabac, too, with only two or three tables and chairs lined up against the wall, and a mirror ran along the wall, reaching to the floor. The woman, perched on the chair, her feet not touching the floor, was half-turned toward the wall, she took a bite at her tartine, leaving behind a white streak of bread in her two clasped hands.

She sat turned away from the rest of the tabac. But she was so small that her round white face hardly appeared in the mirror. She ate like a trapped animal. She did not want to be seen. She did not want to see herself, yet, turning her face away from the space of the tabac, she almost had to be seeing herself, in the mirror, and also in the mirror the inescapable tabac space in which she felt conspicuous.

Or else: she was a very small woman with a round white face which nobody wanted to see, not even herself, but she had to be somewhere, in order to eat. Still, she was eating in such a way as to indicate that she wanted to live, hands clasping bread, even if living meant disappearing.

All around her, all around me, in that small space, the packets of cigarettes and the boxes of matches, the people walking in the street, on their way from the day's work, in their appropriate clothes, and the dogs going about their business, and the continuous roar of all the cars.

Or else: I cannot say all around us. No link. No common root, at best a rhizome, contrived by the other bodies and the noises, in their scatteredness, connected her particularity and mine, within a surface of observation more fleeting even than the last white shred of her tartine at which I saw her now sucking, not chewing, no, but sucking.

The question of her teeth had not yet arisen. Strong teeth, squirrel teeth, grow in straight jaws, but hers might be weak teeth, in such round jaws. She lacked the courage, or else the presumption, to use a good toothpaste, and this had been going on for years. Nor had she the means to visit a dentist. Or else she had once scraped and saved, had once made an appointment, but the dentist had sent her away the moment he saw her. A tartine has a strong crust. So many sacrifices, in such a life. The cheapest food, a tartine, with ham or jam, and a little butter. Even then, she had to eat the tartine in her particular way, by sucking, and in public, she had to turn her face aside and not look, she wanted to eat while being invisible, she had a passion of great force, dangerous, for the tartines of this tabac, and here the rhizome put forth another bud, because in her I saw another being who had to aim, straight-on, for the impossible.

Or else: I went into the tabac after spending an afternoon with a young woman, small and beautiful, with a laugh like the silver trickle of starlight seen in the water of a well. We had walked across bridges and along corridors, we had exchanged sweat from the palms of our hands, we had sat beside one another with mirrors behind us, gazing out into the world, or gazing at each other, in the envious ancient way of Assyrians; but who, now, among the ancient Assyrians would care to wonder about the small woman with the round white face, or who else, one century or two from now, in Paris, would want to know that she existed?

She might never have been touched. I saw her short legs, white and lumpy, because, the way she sat, twisting away from the world, her skirt was hitched up to her knees. Nobody had ever wanted to stroke them. With her weak teeth she had never bitten anybody. With her small and frightened mouth she had never sucked anybody. Or else nobody living one century or

139

two from now, no ancient Assyrian either, would, unless I am mistaken, want or have wanted to be bitten, or else sucked, by the small woman with the round white face and the unstroked legs.

She was not a tiny soldier in the battle against chance, so by chance she had to be a nullity. When she looked in a mirror and saw herself, she might have found it hard to believe that this was all she was: not even worth a glance, but worse—a pretext for averting every glance. Round, small, white zero, with a circumference nobody would dream of stroking into place, thus not even, really, a zero. The continuous roar of traffic. The dogs going about their business. Perched on the chair, a blob of absolute anxiety. Blob—and there they go, the beautiful ancient Assyrians, and others, who can be seen, who think it is they who happen, not chance, who receive existence from a knowledge that they are to be seen; and there they go, the dogs, capering and sniffing, a blob in their track is a small woman with a round white face and wet-looking hair which nobody wants to comb or pat; a blob sucking a tartine in a tabac and looking aside, or else down, she wants only not to be there where everyone else happens to be going.

Or else I am mistaken, entirely mistaken, and what I see is a large and very beautiful flea. A star among the fleas. And the dogs, in holy terror, worship her? From flea to angel, the spectrum of perception bends and cracks under the buffetings of chance, as, in a changed perspective, a world of different objects comes into position. Lens-grinding Spinoza says to the small woman (she does not hear, and I may not have heard correctly): 'Every being which is made conscious of its interior power comes to persevere the more insistently in its particular nature.'

Never once did anything occur to the small woman such as might have shown her that plenitude of interior power. She perseveres because she has been doomed to do so, by the dogs in the street, or else like them, by the space of the tabac, by the mirror which has finally annulled even her capacity to despair of herself. Or else: A chair in a small tabac, her twisted body insisting on it, is this a likely perch for the Celestial Globe-Hopper, the Pure Flea Spirit? Passing from Spinoza's triangle to the cube, I put one box of matches in my coat pocket, the other in my trouser pocket, and could not say whether or not I was mistaken. Or else I had ground this lens not cruelly enough, for I felt mounting in my throat a galaxy of tears; or else I was grinding into the lens not this indelible presence but my own shadow, nicotine, idiotic.

HOW TO LISTEN TO BIRDS

Put no trust in loud sounds
Learn from the crystal
Ladderings of music

To listen: bodily. Slip
Through the rifts which model
Their notes. A moment, one, day
Or night, may be a more favoured
Time

For penetration: one tiny spool
Of the unseen
Unrolls from a chirrup. Feel

Feel again its formal flute alarm,
The wave creation—
A dancing woman's hair, it floats
Across your face—

A note or two, at last,
Concentrates the practised world
Into some new thing

Wake, otherwise, attentive
To such a call, you might
Inhale the first perfume on earth,

Touch the ghost,
Voluminous, of a howl tight coiled
In the plain tune,

Or find no way of your own
To speak
Belief, at a variance so fine
It modifies the whole

Machine of being: this
Is not unpolitical

THE WORLD FIRST

Emptiness, the emptiness in you
Fill it, fill it with, I don't know,
Something, not with toys, not with

Mythologies, fill it
With something, no, you can't, with solid
Villages, or seas, bottle corks, desire,

Inconspicuous bent nails, almost anything,
Fury of enemies, whatever grips
Fill the emptiness for fear

Fill it for never ending
Fill the emptiness or it will tear off heads,
The heads you love, watch them, down the drain

Float like yours, the heads,
Howl and tumble, torn off, not much
Not much to hold on to

Fill the emptiness, facing it, raw grief
Now and really surrounds your face,
Fill it with that, if you can, the world first

And do not dwell on it, laborious, only,
Shapeless hole, seize it, can you,
Scattered curse, you can't blot it out

But clear figures, more than imagine
Other worlds, they spin with other feeling, fill it
Fill it with them, you can't, trackless

No map, impenetrable, specific, you
Can't, but make them dance it out, different,
Muscular and trim, repeat it over and over

Only to yourself, can you now, the emptiness,
Know it inside out, always there,
The great sucking emptiness you keep

Replenishing with towns, the birds, a river,
Roofs of old tiles red and wet with dawn,
You can't, it is always there, control

Impermanent in the timed flight of words
And with your interior animals refresh it,
In first light they do face one another, free

Not spellbound, not,
By the gaze of any remote Upholder,
When for them you invent an open deep indwelling,

Can you, and a secret air, for there you plant
Under the clocks and mouths, under the drums
No foundation without fault, emptiness

Not like this, a turning around, but to be made
Into the holy field of apple trees
If death itself be no more strange or final

HISTORY OF NOT QUITE EVERYTHING

Slamming of a car door outside
Is it you
A burst of music like sea waves human feelings
Turn over and over
Is it you the silvery heat of thigh to thigh

Because my jalopy was radioactive
They took me to the nut house for testing
The hooded lunatics happy as sandboys
Did their dance in a ring

Was it you
Beside me the air with your shape in it
Rustling was it you Hungarian girl with twelve grenades
Went under the tank and blew it to pieces

Between our bodies nothing but the moon stood
Nothing was ever wasted
There was time enough twelve years but was it you
Before I died under a tree we had fallen asleep
Was it you woke up and screamed for a hundred years

And forgotten words who spoke them
Head of a halibut who cut it off
A driftwood stick in sand
Who rammed it into the fish throat from under

Or the provision of justice under law
Is it you
Drenched in blood these were hungry babies
Old men froze by the roadside
Is it you very gentle fingers on the long march

Is it you very gentle fingers
Silent void
The voice
I must go on answering for ever

LENS

The book, blue
Small but thick

Glass ashtray
And the candlestick

A woman's face
On the matchbox

She wears a bonnet
Cypress tree, the tilt

Of a roof and a pink
Mountain peak beyond

Link vaguely
Smile of her mouth

To the curving porcelain
Shallow bowl

Of the candlestick
A swoop and the ashtray

Echoes with clefts to fit
A burning cigarette

As the bowl sits in the brass
Grip of a spindly base

Motions in the depth
Of unastonished stars

Hold such wanderings
Surface to surface

African figurine on a desk
This morning,
Polished with lemon oil, hoists
More high his furrowed hairdo,
Deepens his frown

Abstraction pulls from him a living
Crystal shape, distinct
From books he blinks at; dark wood
Sprang from a tuck in time, but lord
What loops one lives in—

Day's action crushes
The mulberry, then drink at seven,
With one kick bourbon the flamingo
Restores to its native
Air the toothless pink soul

Funny for once it looks, the pit
Of delusion. You wonder at
The skill: what intuition gouged
Three angled dents in his forehead, silver,
Even the tilt of this mouth

Cheek scars plummet to the corners
To force a smile. A nail gores
One eyeball. A sneeze
Might anytime explode. The belly
A column of root—it has returned

His ancient feel for trees
To the whittled beast, worm-eaten
Man. And it is good
When the door creaks open, to find him in
Still, only him.

WILD HORSE

As a more or less literate person
Who writes down things that have
Some connection with the English language

What should I do with a wild horse
Suddenly presenting itself to my thoughts
In Berlin this winter morning

Under no circumstances would I write
About a wild horse in a manner approaching
That of the savage Mr Ted Hughes

I cannot recall that I have ever
Seen a wild horse in the flesh
Perhaps in films but I have not smelled one

Not once not even from afar I have not
Watched a wild horse glow in moonlight
I have never touched one who has?

I do not live in Marlboro Country
I have no spurs no saddle no skill
I cannot even ride a tame horse but this one

This wild horse has given me a shake
Bucking inside me   One moment it is
Chestnut brown like a cello

The next black as Pelikan ink
And white the next like nothing
On earth   Pitiful comparisons

The thing is all muscle and fury
It is controlled as a star is said to be
By certain magnetic conditions

The thing is abrupt   It hears
Who knows what and is off like the wind
In pursuit or going just anywhere

It stops to drink from a pool
Hoofing it over a hill   cropping
Prairie grass   Impulse grips it

This horse but in that grip it is free
Knowing in its bones a radiance
Which I ride like a speck of dust

Bareback   Can the reason be this belt
I bought from a junkstore north of La Grange
Texas?   Its oval bucket with a horse

Embossed on it was first prize once for riding
Bareback in a rodeo   Influences must have
Penetrated my guts gone to my head

Or does it just come at a gallop
This wild horse because a few friends
And loves these past months have

Irradiated my body with something keen
Intrinsic to the universe a power
I would not dream of questioning

Or putting a name to   Don't look down
Or behind   Fly in the fury of the horse
With wild love   They'll drag you off

Soon enough ordinary humdrum things
Is what I tell myself feeling it
And I'm up there all right this very moment

Thinking of you Ann Alberto Caroline
And you Tsëpë Romanian clown my friend
And someone else I'll put no name to

I'm up there all right the world's force
Hits me bends back my spine but hell
Head up I'm going through the crosswinds

Clean with the perfume of Saint Elizabeth's Weed
Or what is it called over the hills and down
Uhlandstrasse   If this is a lion I say hallo

Racoons fling me nuts which I catch
Reaching a hand up as I pass beneath
Cheerful pecans the looped vines the sweet

Sophora   Sun shines all day   Is this
An exaggeration? Probably it is
But this wild horse under me knows best

How to crash through hope the barrier
Shielding the helpless
And how best to help this blaze the universe

Propel itself by subtle shifts
And twistings of the shoulderblades
Onwards   Deep orange canyons then scrub

Flats tender tamarisk cactus towers whizz
Drumming   Its hooves are my heartbeats
Mine its flying sweat silken tail floats out

Into spaces which contract behind us
Bleeding shadows across the kicked dust
At moonrise   To the tinkle of waters

We listen listen the great crag blossoms
Indigo with a hundred faces cut by the ray
From horn and cleft   We watch watch

He appears the magician with his finger
Beckoning the sharp interior form unfolds
Across rock mass   Profile gaze upstream

To where the waters
We now stoop to drink
Have come from

RAZZMATAZZ

δενδρέων δὲ νομὸν Διόνυσος πολυγαθὴς αὐξάνοι
ἁγνὸν φέγγος ὀπώρας.

Pindar, fr. 153 (125)

1

This
Very erect real tree
Sticks in my flesh
And follows it

Through
An eye-swivel
It has grown

A loss of contact
Cement
Wall a sudden house
Blurs

Beyond, perplexing—
All that meat, those lamps—

A heave of twenty branches
Now it shakes off the salt
Rough juice we enjoyed
Again the hole
The hole we pierced

(All heart, or is it)
Fills with a round
Of retreating fictions

O the bleeding hole
Torn in the flesh
      Heart, the hungry people
Beaten down by the winds
  Bayonets, rifle butts

No figure can fill it
    No fiction has healed it
  Do you see them always

The broken souls for whom nobody speaks
And the great birds flying onward

Over the sands that choke
Over the streets that are pitiless

             3

Petals of the sunflower, flames
Lick around
The hole's apparent limit:
A ring of air

Hugs the shivering shapes
Of heat. At noon
Beef starts to sizzle, a calf,
Elsewhere, opens his throat
For a bellow:

Soon the enormous whispering
Forest of fictions
Will assemble to eat:

Afterward, what a collapse: crumple
Sufficient words
Crawl back into your oblong
Nightmare meanings—

No, not so fast:
Inconspicuous
The picked ribs in a bucket
Still make sense, mean business

For our friend Flick Digit
The Flying Guitar

4

Do not lose track. These
Are exercises. Sleepwalking
I make a pattern, see what comes into it
A finger pattern for the smell
Of tree bark, an eye pattern to involve
A taste of gaps

. . . . distance, without focus or history,
I was groping in it
To remake a rainbow. Like that. Impossible
Now listen

What did they have to say
The bloodspeckled messengers always arriving
Why do they have to die
Mesengers who also called the sun silk and yellow
And died gasping 'You don't have time'

In my pattern I wanted
Figures to point without mystification
At themselves, the messengers, on horses half-wild—

Because I am starving, all I can bite on
Are the gasps of messengers as they hit the dust
And I drink the negative stain fast spreading
All over Europe. I wanted

Not the rubber stamping
Punitive bureaucracy of words. The words
Ready in the mouth, what were they to do

On clear skins what act was traced
Simply what were the times they witnessed
What sounded through their veins
In a rhythm of perceiving, before they were told
'Take a chance, ride like fury—
One message is false'

5

What matters is not, I suppose
The hole a figure makes
With tree or sunflower
Through this contracting universe

But the
Hurt: wall, final, unfocussed
You can't push it back, nothing
Can't get me out of here

The human
Round: Who'll build a fruit trap? So many
Wasted works of love—libido's rebound—
Everyone encircling someone,
No air: what was it, space in the veins
Their colour: a joy
To breathe and let breathe

Space—
        Weltinnenraum
                The flying duck
And lions advise me, also Caroline
In her letter:

        On dit qu'en Chine
People have begun to eat one another
Adding:—Paris, all that remains
Is
Remains—
        Of mountain? A rubbish
Pickup *stiften die Dichter*?

Old mountain circle hold up still
The sky's lid, higher

6

No go, that one, can't say
It as it is: the terrible shriek

Of escaping fruits, the numb
Forms, cannibal machines of time

Walking afterward
I was in the tracks we had created
In and out of places where we had stopped

Muse, help me to say what I mean
And this to survive

I entered spaces you had left,
Fitting my body into your hollows
I felt for your hands, your hair

—And me to survive, Muse, I'll need
Every scrap of the folly you've got

It was wild a weeping and a dancing

What is there to catch
But absence, a kind of
Being friends with it. In love's midst
Everything scatters, like birds
At gunpoint

7

Quickly they age, the new spaces

It was, there, the sleep
Mountain, planted with trees like bells
                    Behind the house you saw
Expanding a plateau, in slant light
          Bear and elk and lion

          Tall with legs the giraffe walked
As if a cloud cushioned its breastbone
     And like hope or snowflakes
Five ibis swoop down crossing the blue
                    Screen of trees

               Remote.
From the dust I pick myself up, a few
     Specks of it
Come loose under a fingernail.
          Again I scratch my head, this meat,
Feel.
          How much can hurt in one lifespan

8

          The tentative
                    Figures
     Will not
          Bind up the wound. They are part
Of the great heave, over and over inflicting it
               The splitting of this mind
At that moment when flesh took:
               Over and over the spasm
Repeating itself, birth
               Foredoomed:
          It is man, it is woman

I fish this wound out of time you give me your dream
Siberian midgets backflipping all over the tundra
I give you the wound
You give me a honey cake for my birthday
I give you the wound

You get up and dance when the moon shines in
I teach you the very quick step of the goldfinch
I give you a kiss I give you a wound

You give me a kick and I catch your foot
We twirl to this rhythm you beat out on my back
I give you the wound but whenever it hurts it is there
Where you are not

You give me a little breast I taste you
You taste of mango and Je reviens what a runaround
You give me all it takes I give it back in kind
I give you the first snow a slice of tropical ocean
A grief it was always there I give you the wound

Which suddenly with your fingers you rip open
I scream don't but it is there
The great laugh popping in the wound's root

It comes at us with white teeth
The great laugh shining all over it is truth
I give you wine flute music a flying guitar
Why do you tell me trombones have bald heads
Why do you tell me ghosts smell of egg
I give you the go-by
And if you want it take it, I love you
But what is your name and what name now is mine

I give you, no, this you can only give to yourself
It is a home-made contraption
It fits in nowhere
It is a fruit trap made of air and you

It is made of the wound with the laugh coming out of it
Now mind and flesh join in the song
A whole orchestra ascending
It plays for the fireflies it plays in the wound

You give me a tiny old conversation
It is a little girl in red lace pantaloons
I give you a glass photo of freedom

What I cannot give you call it what you will
By small names for it is passionate and without fear
When it goes out there to do it look it escapes
Because it is so passionate
It might multiply the infliction of wounds

It is not often at home among human concerns
It is not really at home on earth at all
Not in the Guadalupe Mountains not in New Orleans
Not in Calcutta not in South Dakota where is it

Where it is
Happens between, happens between names
When I call you by yours feel it
Call me by mine believe me back I shall come

THE TURQUOISE

Somehow the memories fizzle out on us.
Large blank eyes of people starving.
A snatch of music soon
Will be Merida, the mirrored bedroom, not
The pang felt there, but a fountain
Touches palm trees. Pang—

I forgot how perception had to be
Wrenched from its
Regular socket: the speech of folds, eyewhite
And snow the robe a woman wore,
Foreign liquor
The smell of a man at noon in his hammock.

Raw stuff: a crooked
Line of objects. Look, it is put
Straight like hair by distance.
The whole shadow of (our tune) your smile
Oozed first from
Repetition on a jukebox. Careless

Memory cooks
The kind of meal you
Gulp down, because the right place
Had shut, or the old prices are
Out of sight. Compulsion
Turns you still

Back to the same town: the flies
In children's eyes are blue, the drowned
Horse prongs the air still,
Silver hoof; never sensing wrong,
The deadly salesmen frisk again
With girls in the disco.

Swot a fly, scratch the wall
Of an ear with a toothpick: four, suddenly,
The grouped figurines
Loom huge from the desk angle,
And glow, clay Chupicuaro, bronze
Krishna, the wooden African—

As gods. To construct them
Ancestors broke through their skins,
Getting this far at least: the rock
Crystal coyote, stud him
With turquoise, let the orange fire
Be a tail like a beacon;

For the unseen escapes,
The remembered
Dominion cracks, falsifies
Desire and presence as they fly screaming
Before us, headdress and tail
Bushy, slashing backward in the dark.

OLD WATER JAR

Like one of the old ideas
It won't hold water any more
But it is round in the belly
And has strong bladed
Shoulders like a good woman
Elegant even the curves
Run down from the mouth
In a long sweet wave
You can't help liking it so
Simply for the way
It stands there

A ROAD THAT IS ONE IN MANY

for George and Mary Oppen

This is a little road, this part of it
Like the centre bar of an old hand drill
Runs straight from this bend to the next

Hold tight when you walk along it
Violet orbs revolve under the pebbles,
Daily shadows. These vines have grapes

Shrub vines, bitter grapes, mustang. Hold tight
When this bird spider hauls his thick ass
Over the tarmac, this pothole is his

Hold tight to your straight walk, tiptoe
Certain spots are swept by heat
That is what blows, that is what dries

The inside of your mouth. The signs
Droop or rust, are not adequate
To the events they warn about. Warn

The pecan comes late into leaf, the big
Pecan; that is juniper, a cone, house
Of a singing bird. The signs do not sing

Being, but collisions, they take sometimes
A life or two. Hold tight, don't roll off, all
Sorts of people have walked along this road

This road is old, new, was Indian trail
By water, TU, they said, water; now
Corvettes and subarus, few foot people

This field in summer clings to a thatch
Of slow dragonflies; now nothing lives
In the tin shed, or is it nothing, only

Bugs, but you can moo to the ghosts
Of seven extinct preoccupying cows. Not
A slope in sight. These black

Eyed susans are the prettiest flower,
Later the dayflower marks its own distinct
Fluting off against this sky of skies

And the white rain, the white rain lilies
Really are these fragrant acid fruits
Of rain. Soon it stops. Under the polestar

At night hold tight still, grip this
Ground with your unshackled feet,
Don't scare these vines or ghosts are

Vines and ghosts. At night the lake
Is good for a swim. Don't mind these bats
That flit crisscross close to the cooling

Surface. Hold tight just once again,
Then let go and be consumed by the cool.
This is in the things and shines in the things.

PINYON INCENSE

Oblong a pellet
In a small
Pueblo bowl

Careful
It could come to bits
A fleck like conscience

Burn as you light
One tip
And breathe on it a pang

Possibly a finger
Writing but
A fresh piece

And firm shoots mysterious blue
Scented smoke up
If ever the smoke thins

Look while ash
Blackens the tip it is
Not standing on

Down through the spirals move
Meet
Old man trombone brown

He stands
Where his feet keep him
At a cave opening

Watch the writ of furrows
Groove his dry
Pine bark

Palm he is
Not angry now he simply will not
Let you in

With your sorrow
And your bodyful of pacts
Broken

Let him say
Sorrow let him say
Nothing

Just cup like that his
Palm and cuff
The top of your head off

PEOPLE IN KANSAS, 1910

1

Now they stand quite still on level doorsteps,
Outside the Drug Store and the Post Office.

A white sky, two buildings underneath it,
Outside the buildings half a dozen people.

Across the dust like dice the buildings rolled,
Stopped under the white sky.

Soon the people prised them open, clambered out.
Here at last. Here, they said, is Dorrance.

2

Stiff, like effigies, almost,
Made of language; speaking
The people came to be real for one another.

A head below the P of the Post Office
Shrinks into a Stetson. A wiry woman
Shoulders the stone Drug Store doorpost.

All six like effigies, wax, mechanical.
Work all day with corn, beans, soda pop.
The letters, few and far between. Senseless.

3

The people insist. But a vague terrain—
How can you fill it. Corn and letters
Stop short. The horizon,

A banker might one day darken it,
Locomotives. This big space frightens. We
Lost here a sense of belonging with the wind,

Now geese and trees that fly with it are no part of us.
Trust your shirt, these oblong blocks of stone.
Trust two dark heaps dropped in the dust by horses.

A chimney pot, back of the Post Office. Plain
Undistressed people, you never dreamed
Of burning letters, one by one, or bodies.

That's it. None could know what later crooked
Shapes
History takes when something radiant
All the brain and body cells cry out for
Is suppressed.

Behind bars appetites riot; captured
Guards
Sob for mercy; spies are fucked.
These oblong people lived out their free time
On credit,

They could count it wise not to wish
Their soap
Were sweeter, small business not
So methodical, dogs happy to work
Nights for them.

No. Their stark speech I do not understand.
Why
Make of life such a hard nut?
Or did they? Far off, faceless, kin of mine,
Hard living

Salt of the earth, sharply defined, crystal
Flakes,
You were never as oblong
As the buildings that warmed and warped you.
You weren't fooled.

5

Focus again,
So sharp you can smell the cigar,
The string beans taste
Just right. Objects, it
Was not your fault, objects, if
That is what you were, you have to go

164

Forth, shoulder your signs
In capital letters, onward to a place
I tell you of,
A place of blue and yellow. There
Mountains and people are one indivisible creature,
A grape admits night glow
To become its body,

Absolute, good as the bread
Is dense to the teeth
With death and legend. There, with patience
And the scent of sage,
People other than you ripened once
To a style—some to foreknow
And resist evil. Goodbye

Innocent oblongs, forget nothing
Now it is too late, but
Forget my fist with which if I could
I'd bang this postage stamp through
Into the reversed
World you stand in. It

Would stick in your sky of whiteness,
Perforated, a script of waves,
Muttering to you,
A voice, cancelled:
The sun does not shine for anyone,
The leaf arrives one breath
Only before the wind.

AN OLD WINE PRESS

1

An old wine press
With its iron screw
Column down the middle—
Vertical slats doubly hooped
Contain the tub—this instrument
Sepia on account of its being
Not the very thing but a photo dated
No later than 1910

2

Higher up, steep slant of a barn roof.
The line of its eave like a lip,
Wavy. A sort of monster
Grin goofily reveals
The stubs of seven teeth, unless
These are beam ends or swallows' nests

3

And halfway up the slant
Two holes are built, like little eyes, or else
They breathe for the hayloft, handy
Homes of dove, dark lodges
For the grape scented air

All this no more than a glimpse
But the barn behind the wine press caught
And carries onward
A human imprint, rough hewn
A flicker of the torch

Here for once
Doubly precious, considering these
Eight people grouped around the press:

Just a bunch of farm folk, three generations,
The men clothed in stained denims, sweaty caps;
The woman has pinned a flower to her breast
And holds an empty cheese basket;
A little boy had curled his fingers
Around the handle of a hooped
Wooden wine jug

6

There they stood, tilting
Every which way; splay feet, beefy arms
Dovetailed into a right good
Angular design:

          Three men
Lean against the tub on its platform;
If this beard might crumple into a king's mask,
Still clog and boot crack with mud
And glue these
Dancers to the ground; the boy
Hangs in the middle, perched, dangling
Tiny booted feet—

Any moment
The glass he grips by the stem will spill;
Oddly tender yet, the way
All around him thicker fingers hold
The scarce seen cool substance—
In it gleams the god, red and savage,
Spinning the world for more than money

7

Yet the money matters. You can plot
Grim pursuit of it in the skew
Cheek folds of the white-haired man.
Hope made the woman's mouth
A thin long line and in her round chin
Totted up
Credits of hair, winnings of eye, decimals
Of nostril

8

Who knows, it is mostly too late;
The wine that time at least
Had a fair chance;
The footwear might see another ten years out,
As good as a second skin, these denims
Are worn as the sun
Wears its light, or as the god they nourish
Squid-wickedly has thrown
History over his tentacles, a robe
Smoky in colour, a tissue of bloodstains,
Whose, fading, sepia

IRISH

Here as the bamboo
leaf and rod
glisten
in broken moonlight
this harp music

I suppose it echoes
the strings of rain, silver
those dark pools
drink up
on streets in Ireland

Say time could have taken
a different shape,
but this, with red eyes that weep
and search the horizon
choose we did

Say a spirit got
knotted
in spilt intestines, a body
of music shattering
the bamboo door

Now leaf and rod
the fawn I saw stopped
in a clearing, pulsars in moth-
eaten velvet
flash slow beacons

But a perception chosen
digs historic
claws deep down, not
like the bamboo rhizomes
they touch dancing

Pickled
in this whiskey bottle was
a heart, do not listen
the wind sings in its
ventricle, seaward

AFTER A NOISE IN THE STREET

It is the small
Distinct image, old as you like,
On a coin, or silvery
In a daguerreotype

Speaks to me:
The trooper Probus,
Two centimetres high, at most,
Helmeted, sloping

A spear
Across a shoulder,
Condenses all
The gas of empire

Into a few
Quick signs. No fuss, either,
Had perplexed her face,
This young and tawny

Woman, but
An anger, fine, makes
Luminous now the eyes
She levelled in Nebraska

At the lens, never
Exhausting it, for the hands
Folded and slender in her lap
Siphon a torrent

Of feeling through the image.
There is anguish
Untrapped, an ardent
Breath sets free to fall

A dew as on a cherry,
To magnify, by sharpening
So far, the resolute
Infinitesimal flesh, this wisp

Of being, only this
A mortal
Tentatively manifests. A
Measure just

One fraction grander could
Put back
Into the spear
Slaughter;

Distend a pleat
In this dress, or blow
A tassel up
Beyond belief—and it lumbers

Back into the flimflam; an
Embossed cuirass,
Probus any bigger, snagged
In power's mesh

Spills, as a blur, or boast,
His contracted time
Into the heaving
Primordial pettiness.

Sir, I do not know your name,
Nor do you know mine. So we sit,
Briefly, at neighbouring tables, you
With your bottle, the cat on your knee,
I with my little glass.

In our sunken ship
The third table has been taken
By the fine man of darkness, whom
We do not see. Look, on the furrowed surface
Glittering still, the flake of snow I flicked
From the collar of my coat when I came in.

Each sits watching
The face of his own slowly turning
Universe. Particularly the cat
Has known how the heat
Comes and goes. Important smells
Wrinkle and flex into signatures, you know,
Writ small in snowflakes and the skeletons
Of leaves. Shuddering,
The fingers of a spirit ink into our skins
Mysterious names, numbers, and messages.

Ancient gutters
Accommodate the cat, providing
Fish, spare ribs, a scrap of lamplight;
Spilt milk to lap up, now and then.

There are places where people turn yellow,
Having nothing to eat. Cloacas, attics.
Broken roofs. Through holes the snow sifts.
A Valois song can be issuing, in another street,
From a little girl's lips
For a penny.

Mandolins, a lantern swaying, make it
Difficult to want less than a tree to dance with.
Do we suffer
Most because the bunched worms will hang
In the emptiness you are looking at, this
Dome of mine, bald, this bony cabin?
                              What is immortal
If not the injustice?

There was a room I lived in once,
I remember how the early light in it
Fell across two rescued Fragonards.
There was a girl, nearly naked she was,
Tigers ran before her on a leash
And a little donkey woke us, braying,
Or a barge trumpet's echo off the river.

Like a swift in his globe of crisp mud
I hung between sleep and waking
And heard the straw speak in my thin
Mattress. Look, here it is, another face
Of that same
Towering light, again
In this bit of a rainbow, at its peril
Afloat in the eau-de-vie:
I drink it for the dream that spills
Into life.

They tore it down, it was an old house.
They did not tear down
The other room, which, if you follow me,
We put there, suspending it
Outside any space that iron balls
Can shatter.

In that room the last vine still grew,
A veiny green, very ancient.
The last vine, first planted when
The emperor was Julian and Paris Egypt.
From the vine,
Yes from it you might see
A light as from the original stars unfolded

173

And flew as it pleased, to vary
As it touched the featured walls through
Twelve emotions. With snaky lines
It marbled the stones and old chairs
We had broken by leaning back to laugh.
To eye the stones was to feel a flow
Of female warmths and hear the goddess,—
Moan and shriek of the sistron in her fingers.

What can you be thinking?
No, do not indispose the cat.

FAR-FROM-HOME POEM

1

A far-from-home poem
Foolish you can't put it together
The fingers tremble
A glistening cave in the guts
Fills with bats very eager for flight
Cries of children come from the sky
Little mouths everywhere open

2

It is not the place that calls like this
The place calls in its own fashion
With a smell of cedar smoke in early light
Transparent emerald

It calls with the buzzard
Seen above oaks and circling
As you lie in a hammock naked
It calls with the bodies of things
A little statue a Roman lamp a waterpot
You gathered up for they outlive you

4

Lake in the morning see fish
Flit through luminous shallows
Bird call cutting outline
On sky nothing but bird call
Nothing you can put a sense to

5

A clean sheet once in a while
Calls
And waking to enfold in your arms
A being who still dreams and kicks you
Says don't stop my dream

6

Not much of a roof as the sun
Hacks it into crinkles
And the rain calls
And the pipes that are stopped with roots
And the animals I mean wild ones

7

With curiously spelled names
Like you are for a while their neighbours
You dare to intrude

8

If only the snakes were more ferocious
If only the insects were worse
What a call you might hear
The terrible clamour of wings the orchestra of fangs
Snapping

9

As it is the bamboo just clicks
Clatters when the wind blows at moonrise
And the catbird calls in it
To the dog who is hungry
Mocking

RILKE'S FEET

1

Heart bowels hand head and O the breast
So many of the parts fan out
Pressing on speech
Each a shape distinct
At length delivered a message
Classified sensitive

2

Perched in my tree as the light
Tries to unfold over Wilmersdorf

Rilke's feet a phrase
Ran amok in the mass below—

But in the grass
Not a trace left—playing

Woodland god he walked there
Barefoot—before architecture

Boiled the green to stone gray—
1897: I had taken my shoes off . . .

3

Sweetheart, Lou

. . . what is God, Mama?

> "White hinds
> hidden in a thorn thicket"

No compliment to the long
Undulant chevelure of Magdalen

On a billow of mud
     in the Dordogne or Ariège was it
A footmark printed
     lightly
Hard mud in a deep cave

Might last another 15,000 years

But Rilke's feet
     he left them
          standing
To be invented

This hot pursuant of
The Incomparable

A sort of hassock stool
He kept and kneeling on

Upholstered velvet
Worshipped any woman

He had invited no
Not any but this

Was the way he tended
Kneeling on the stool

And gazing up as
She waved an arm or

Cringed and bit her lip
Footless for some quaint

Antiphallocratic reason he
Poised at hers

A projectile
In a catapult

5

Or Rilke had no feet at all
What he had was fins
Up he twiddles into the air

Sycamore seed going the wrong way
Lands in my tree
Owl's eyes large liquid

Blink at me   Contrariwise
He had no body just a head
Thought a little girl

No body in his clean but threadbare
Clothes crossed the room
And took a cake with Mama later

Off again
Somehow bowing
Where can he have put that cake?

6

More famous feet
Than these invisible ones
The foot of Philoctet-
Es and Byron's

Hoof with its iambic knock
On the deck of a gondola,
Incidentally—copper,
His horse adored the hot

Weight of it and ladies
Lifted fingers to their eyes,
Thrilling stomachs
Fancy the surprise

Suddenly milord is dead
While muttering Greek
Bandits around his bed
Frenetically seek

To screw the damn thing off,
Here's Philoctetes' foot
Festering in a cave—
His wound minute by minute

Throbs away the years,
Four thousand of them spin
Till Troy falls to hexameters
And Rilke's feet begin

7

A Wicked One
When he scraped the Many
Bits together
Must have made some funny faces

Rilke's feet—how
Is this body
To be looked upon: a

Screen or
Not sure a
Scene a recipient interim

And liminally
In and over it creation's
Wavering shapes break open
Yet

Are distorted it is
The dance but done
As if by hangmen

Touch and look
From a footsole run
Tightrope lines to every single organ

8

Voice where are you now
Tree what has become of you
Never a column or pedestal

But a tree of branching blood vessels
A tree trying to speak
Through thunderous pumping of juices
I climb across this voice
In the grip of its twig deletions

9

Hands whose touch is thinking
  How the taste of orange flows
To the beat of a ringdance

Slowly out of its givens
  The automatic body
Builds itself

Might balance feet with
  Strong straight
Articulations but dammit

An orchestra of echoes
  Code of interchanging
Trait and ancestor

All we can see in one photo
  Is Rilke in
Well shone shoes with spats

Its constant monologue
  Broken by torture
Reroutes no signals

And a shoe might hide
  One discord perhaps a hand
Froze an insurgent impulse

And clogs
  In the negative
I am told

Now like an undesired
    Eyeball captive in a pod of skin
For fingers wished it

Footward as a pipesmoker
    Tamps tobacco
Down to the base of the pipe bowl

So blue huggermugger knobs
    When bones obtrude strum on tendons
Fuming toes

Recoil to plot
    Inversion of the message
Train to be fingers and pluck back

Their slice of the power
    Did Rilke then support a claw
Brain-limb feedback

Did it flush his touch of sphinx
    Faintly at the tip
With repression's rose

10

Rilke's feet
Wading in a weird
Kettle of fish

       The lobster
Has gone for a walk
With his ghost
The sea
Once
Too often

11

Xenophon Xenophon it were fit to include
Dark as it is again in Wilmersdorf
An echo of your script from Corinth, your
Fictional grammar of the human foot

Anabasis uh I am tired and my secret
Reader wonders where we have got
As did your mob of Greeks thirty years before
Thirty years before you finally wrote

A bit boastfully about the march to the sea
Then how your lines inch by inch
Barrelled along the barbarous coast

But hardly anyone cares now
About the fleetfooted Carduchi
Peltists and bowmen coming up quick

When they shoot they put the left foot out
And rest the base of the bow on it
Drawing back the string

You must have stopped to see that

And soon backwards the snow
Is opening its white tomb

Illshod columns of infantry
Straggle into Armenian mountains
Was there no shit they could not bite through

Newly flayed oxenskin
Froze that night to the footsoles
Thongs cut into ankle flesh

Many perished
Snowblind thwacking spear on shield
Throat racket body racket made the foe
Feel outnumbered

Small bags later we tied
To the horse hooves else
In the snow to their bellies they sank

12

Can I speak to you now Rilke
As we sleep
A little for our lives
Though I wonder sometimes what you meant
And my memory is awful
The footless motions you enact or track

In poems where the verbs
Amaze by their precision
Were you pointing
Beyond the combative body which engulfs
All as nothing with its bubble

Pointing to a body more like music
A luminous relator with its warmth
"Transfiguring the earth"
If it was this what have we got
Not evil quite wondrous desires
But injustice

It may be too late
Your invisible
Feet can do nothing but insist
Issue into a space all
Rondure and volume void

Of anything more dense
Than the thrum of air you felt
Around a seagull's wing
As it poured the pearliness in
And fitted feathers

Threadless motion
Through it your truant feet
Sprinkling punctures might
Sustain
Like intervals between them utterly

Determined throngs of stars
Or freely quickening and distinct
These feet it is
That ease
The gasps of joy from children's throats